ISLA VISTA:
A CITIZEN'S HISTORY

by Carmen Lodise
& Friends

A project of Isla Vista Ink.

More information at: www.islavistahistory.com

Cover design by Genesis Augustine Lodise

Front cover photograph from the Isla Vista *Free Press*.

ISBN: 1434824748
EAN-13: 9781434824745

Printed in the United States of America
CreateSpace Publishing edition / January 2009

10 9 8 7 6 5 4 3 2

PREFACE

How is Isla Vista to be remembered by the literally hundreds of thousands of people who have lived there and to be viewed by the hundreds of thousands more to come?

It is definitely a unique place, but is it something special?

I've always thought so. What follows are some of my recollections of the events and institutions that tell the story of the Isla Vista I came to know.

This is not the only viewpoint on Isla Vista but it is an honest portrayal of the 20 years I spent there (1972-92) as a community activist during a period many people call the best of times, and then another dozen years on special projects.

From an era that everyone involved knew had such incredible potential, Isla Vista today drifts in the disarray of ineffective rule by the County of Santa Barbara and the University of California, Santa Barbara and it has turned out to be a bumpy ride for all concerned. Despite the heartbreak of failed campaigns, the clarity of the vision remains of a vital, clean-energy town based on mutual respect among its citizenry and run electorially by a perpetually youthful majority selected from the brightest young people California has to offer.

This history was first self-published on newsprint in 1990 as a 64-page booklet that was banned at the UCSB Bookstore. It was launched April 26, 2002 as a website, with Genesis Augustine Lodise as the principle webmaster. The website averaged over 600 hits/day for many years and passed a total of 1.6 million hits in mid-2008. Many photographs and charts have been added to this book version, plus there have been some minor corrections in text and some major updating of some of the stories.

In November 2008, the Isla Vista Recreation & Park District put on the ballot a measure that would have permitted the board of directors to sell the subterranean rights to the town's central parks in order to build an underground parking lot. See pp. 127-28. Whereas the measure required a 2/3rds majority vote by the electorate, it was defeated nearly 3-1. The trouncing of this absurd plan just might be the spark to usher in a new era of great opportunities for this remarkable town.

Carmen Lodise
Barra de Navidad, Mexico
January 2009

DEDICATION

This book is dedicated to all of those who have fallen under the spell of

the Isla Vista Adventure.

ACKNOWLEDGMENTS

Many of these stories first found their way into print
with the help of
Gordon Harsaghy, Dr. Dave, Rosie
and the advertisers and investors in the Isla Vista *Free Press*.

This book could not have been completed
without the assistance of
Genesis Augustine Lodise
and Sally Derevan.

Thank you to the UCSB *Daily Nexus* and the Santa Barbara *News-Press*
for permission to use several photographs that first appeared in those publications.
Also to Robert Bernstein for his photos of June 10, 2003.

And thank you to the Hal Leonard Publishing Co.
for permission to print the lyrics to
Neil Young's song "Ohio,"
for which I gladly paid $100.

But no thanks to the Alfred Publishing Co.,
which denied the use of the lyrics to
the Rolling Stones' song "Street Fighting Man" at any price.

And no thanks to the Santa Barbara County Sheriff's Department
for its refusal to provide Isla Vista crime statistics for the years 1998 and 2007.

What can I say?

TABLE OF CONTENTS

Maps of Isla Vista
showing its relationship to California, Santa Barbara, and Goleta
SOURCE: <u>Recommendations for Isla Vista Planning</u> (1973)

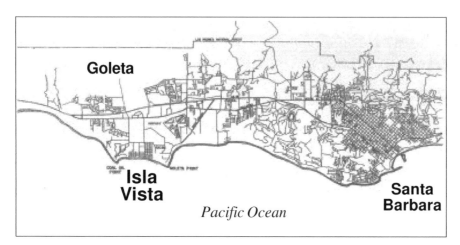

INTRODUCTION

THE CAMPUS BY THE SEA

The "Campus by the Sea" [the University of California, Santa Barbara] had from its beginnings been an unusual combination of academic elements. Its students, though drawn from the upper 12% of California high school graduates, gave the appearance of being more leisure oriented and less academically motivated than students at other UC campuses. The faculty, for its part, was split between a cadre of older professors from the earlier liberal arts college days and an infusion of young research-oriented Ph.D.'s from major graduate schools who were expected to determine the institution's future. The Administration, preoccupied with building programs, looked confidently ahead to the day when UCSB would match Berkeley and UCLA in prestige, enrollment, and academic diversification.

This photo is from Ray Varley's book, Isla Vista U.S.A. (1970).

By 1968, when UCSB had already become the third largest UC campus in terms of enrollment, it was clear that these diverse elements were in the process of changing. But these changes did not bring a harmonious evolution into a prestigious major university, as had been hoped. Instead, they brought students, faculty, and Administration increasingly into conflict, mutual distrust, and finally confrontation.

The Campus by the Sea Where the Bank Burned Down., p. 14
A Report on the Disturbances at the University of
California, Santa Barbara and Isla Vista, 1968-70
Submitted to the President's Commission on Campus Unrest
at the request of Commissioner Joseph Rhodes, Jr.
Written and edited by Robert A. Potter and James J. Sullivan.

At the beginning of the 1960s, Isla Vista was a sleepy college town two hours north of Los Angeles, which was surrounded on three sides by the University of California, Santa Barbara and on the fourth by the Pacific Ocean. Crowded toward the west end of this half-square-mile rural area were several dozen beach houses while herds of cows and goats roomed its open fields. Even as Isla Vista's vacant lots began sprouting duplexes and multi-story apartment buildings built to house UCSB's rapidly expanding enrollment (from 2,879 in 1959 to 13,733 in 1969), surfing and sunbathing remained its

major leisure-time activities well past the middle of the decade. A football team came and went as the outlook and appearance of students changed dramatically toward the end of this pivotal decade, the result of both national and local events.

Gradually a UCSB degree was becoming more valuable and Isla Vista became widely known as a fun place both to study and to play.

The center of nightlife in I.V. was the Magic Lantern Theater (now UCSB's Isla Vista Theater) with its attached book store, which were owned by Ken Maytag, a grandson of the washing machine builders, and Borsodi's Coffeehouse, across the street on Trigo Rd. initially, but later across the street from the Bank of America.

The Magic Lantern ran the most radical and hip movies available, and many of them for weeks or months at a time at midnight showings on weekends. "The Battle of Algiers" and later "The Rocky Horror Picture Show" were each shown over 100 times, according to one observer.

Although Isla Vista is only ten miles from downtown Santa Barbara, until the mid-1990s hundreds of acres of open fields and marshlands separated it from the sprawling

Well past the middle of the 1960s, surfing and sunbathing were the most popular liesuretime activities in Isla Vista. This photo is also from Ray Varley's book, Isla Vista U.S.A. (1970), as are all pictures in this chapter unless noted otherwise. Varley was an assistant dean of students at the time his book was published. He soon left UCSB, taking a similar positon at another western university.

suburbs of Goleta to the north and west. At the beginning of the 1970s, there was no public transportation in or out of Isla Vista, no public services, and only one park, which was on the beach in the west end.

As Potter and Sullivan pointed out (p. 5), the town had many of the characteristics of an urban ghetto: it was isolated, it had a transient population with a housing stock over 95% absentee-owned, and there was a startling lack of street lights and sidewalks.

But there was free live music offered up by local musicians several days a week in a vacant lot in the center of town known as Perfect Park, although the music had definitely taken on some attitude by the end of the '60s.

At one time, murals covered almost all exterior walls in Isla Vista's commercial district. This psychedelic one -- in orange, pink, and tan -- was on the south wall of what became Borsodi's Coffeehouse in 1973. Photo from the Isla Vista Slide Show.

Linda and Robert Borsodi in the mid-70s. Borsodi's Coffeehouse opened in the late '60s at 6529 Trigo Rd. It moved to 938 Embarcadero del Norte (now Javan's) in 1973, across from the re-built Bank of America fortress, now UCSB's Embarcadero Hall. With live music and good, cheap food, it was Isla Vista's unofficial community center until it closed in 1988. This picture, by an unknown photographer, first appeared in the Isla Vista *Free Press* in 1988.

By this time, over 13,000 people lived in Isla Vista's cramped quarters, roughly 9,000 of them UCSB students. But the town had 4,000 "continuous drug users," according to the local sheriff. So despite the military draft waiting to gobble up any young man not enrolled in university, Timothy Leary's proclamation to "Tune In, Turn On, Drop Out" played well in Isla Vista, as it did in college towns across the country.

As Charles Reich pointed out in his bestselling book The Greening of America (1971), the use of marijuana and other psychoactive drugs was changing how many young people looked at the world.

Isla Vista's Perfect Park about 1970. Located at the top of the loop where the three Embarcaderos meet, this was the town's central park until Anisq'Oyo Park opened in 1976. See Chapter 12 regarding how the community eventually acquired it.

Without really knowing why, they discarded bras and grew their hair long, increasingly delineating themselves from the world of "straights."

Soon the anti-war speeches, delivered between songs in Perfect Park, drew larger and larger crowds. The music itself grew more edgy, reflecting the new worldview being revealed almost daily by such ultra-popular poets as the Jefferson Airplane, Rolling Stones, Crosby, Stills, Nash & Young, and, of course, Bob Dylan. These bards created a whole new genre, which blended love and revolution.

Madrid Road, looking toward the UCSB campus (note Storke Tower in the upper left) and the back end of the Bank of America building a few weeks before it was burned to the ground on February 25, 1970. This section of Madrid Road is where Anisq'Oyo Park is today.

Having come of age in a time of empire and environmental degradation, yet filled with the hope

Isla Vista Slide Show photograph.

informing their music and New Age literature, these young people began systematically challenging the belief systems they had inherited from their parents and teachers, ironically the so-called "greatest" generation that had won WWII.

Addressing the most glaring injustices and inspired by the successes of the Civil Rights Movement, college students began asking for more relevant courses of study. Although it took a lot of struggle and many arrests, the University eventually added a one-course requirement in ethnic studies.

However, more was needed than simply rejecting the old ways; people need guidelines for everyday living. The methodology of seeking new values in experience – pleasurable experience — ranks right up there in revolutionary times. So it is that when humans in large numbers look inward for instruction, as they did in the 1920s and other time-bending epochs, they tend to find sex as

The 1st Annual Isla Vista Nude In, May 1, 1970. This free-for-all event was traditionally held on the beach at the foot of El Embarcadero Rd. Isla Vista Slide Show photograph.

their guide ("If it feels good, do it!" was a popular mantra during all of this "greening"). The new birth control technologies made this direction all the more likely an option.

There are few things as sexual as dancing in front of a live band or marching in a really good demonstration.

Sexual liberation, nudity, even pornography were big hits across this country and most other industrialized nations during that period, driving a big wedge between these societies and the defenders of more traditional ones. But it also drove a wedge between this new generation and the more traditional elements of American society, a dividing line that lives on even into the 21st Century.

Thus, there's no denying that it was sex, drugs and rock 'n' roll that were at play in Isla Vista at the end of the 1960s, just like they were the major ingredients in college towns across the country. However, what else was going on in Isla Vista to explain how things got so out of hand?

This is a story about an populist uprising, the very public examination of its causes, the community that arose from the trenches of a dysfunctional town, and its continued saga. But let's first examine the development of the physical setting that was widely seen as the catalyst for the great conflagration of 1970.

CHAPTER 1

FROM INDIAN SETTLEMENT TO STUDENT GHETTO

The Spanish came to what is now southern Santa Barbara County in the mid-1500s. An almost psychedelic four-walled mural depicting the first meeting of the Chumash and the Spanish conquistadors, painted in the 1920s by Dan Sayre Groesbeck, is on the second floor of the Santa Barbara County Courthouse building.

What the Spanish found was a thriving tribe of Chumash Indians thought to number 10,000 or more, living along the coast from the present town of Camarillo north to Morro Bay. The Chumash were known for their seagoing abilities. They even inhabited the Channel Islands, where remains of human habitation are some of the oldest in North America.

The Chumash were a peaceful people, living in grass huts along the shoreline. They used jimson weed (*datura*) ceremonially and their cave paintings, consisting mostly of mandelas, are quite impressive. The most accessible paintings can be found in on Painted Cave Road, just off San Marcos Pass (St. Rt. 154), less than 15 miles from Isla Vista.

Spanish explorer Juan Cabrillo coming ashore in Santa Barbara in 1542, in a detail of a four-walled mural located in the Santa Barbara County Courthouse. The mural was painted in 1928 by Dan Sayre Groesbeck.

Large Lagoon

There was a major community of Chumash at the edge of Isla Vista around a large lagoon. This lagoon once covered what is now the Santa Barbara Municipal Airport, stretching west almost to Storke Road, and south across El Colegio Road. It was deep enough to be navigable by early Spanish and English two-masted schooners (*goletas* in Spanish). Many historians believe that Sir Francis Drake stopped here in 1579, losing an anchor that was found about 100 years ago and perhaps even some cannons discovered more recently. Jasper de Portola was another early visitor to this lagoon.

The Chumash community was centered on an island in the lagoon that at one time held over 100 homes and 800 inhabitants. There were several other villages around the edge of the lagoon and the Spanish

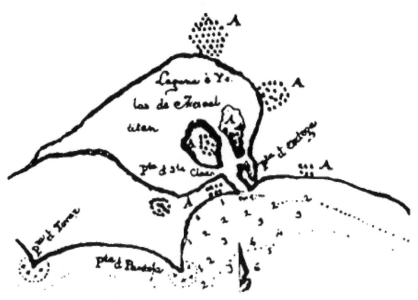

Mescalitan Lagoon from a 1782 drawing. More than 1,000 Chumash Indians lived on the islands in this lagoon and in villages spread around its edges before the arrival of the Spanish in the mid-1500s. The two promontories on either side of Isla Vista (Coal Oil Point to the west and Goleta Point to the east) are both clearly visible in this drawing. Heavy rains in 1862-63 transformed the lagoon into swampland and during World War II, the U.S. Navy bulldozed the remaining hills into what remained of the swamp to create a military airport.

called all of these "Mescalitan." Mescalitan Island was a prominent landmark until 1941 when the Army Corps of Engineers leveled it to provide fill for a Marine air base.

To the Chumash, "Anisq'Oyo" was an oak-covered, coastal mesa between the villages along the lagoon and the ocean, which is Isla Vista today, including the UC Santa Barbara campus. While they did not locate their huts in Anisq'Oyo, they did use the tar still found on its beaches as caulking for their ocean-going canoes.

Isla Vista has retained a connection to the Chumash period through naming its central park Anisq'Oyo.

Although considered to be one of the largest and most culturally advanced Indian populations along the Pacific Ocean, only a few hundred Chumash survived the Spanish Period (1567-1822). In addition to the devastation of European diseases, the Chumash were typically enslaved, turning out candles and blankets that were exported to the far reaches of the Spanish Empire. La Purisma Mission near Lompoc, about 50 miles west and north of Isla Vista, is a particularly graphic example of the economic/military lifestyle of the Spanish era.

Dos Pueblos

During the Mexican Territory Period (1822-46), the Isla Vista mesa was an obscure portion of the 15,000-acre Rancho de los Dos Pueblos, a Mexican land grant given to Nicholas Augustus Henry Den from Mescalitan Island to Las Llegas Canyon, and from the ocean up into the foothills.

But in 1862, things suddenly changed. The heaviest rain ever to hit California began in November and continued for over three months. The runoff from the rain caused a major, permanent change in the area by filling in the lagoon, creating what is now the Goleta Slough. During the rain, Den became ill and died in early 1863. Following his death, there was a major reversal in the weather, with the worst drought anyone could remember. By the end of 1864, the majority of their cattle had died and the Den heirs sold off most of their land, retaining only the Isla Vista mesa. This was soon divided between two sons, and on the dividing line was planted a row of eucalyptus trees. That row of trees currently marks the boundary between the UCSB Main Campus and Isla Vista and is often referred to as the "Eucalyptus Curtain," denoting the vast socio-economic differences between the campus and the town.

Early Economic Ventures

In the 1870s, whaling ships frequently camped just east of UCSB's Main Campus on what is now Goleta Beach County Park. The Den brothers rented their ranch to the More brothers, who cut down the oak forest on the Isla Vista mesa and sold the wood to the whalers, who used it for boiling kettles of whale blubber. The consequence was that the topsoil was lost and Isla Vista was left with only blow sand.

A drawing of a Chumash village from the book California's Chumash Indians (1988). For more information on the Chumash Indians, visit the Santa Barbara Natural History Museum.

Another commercial venture of that period was the mining of asphalt. The Alcatraz Asphaltum Mining Corporation dug several underground shafts on the present Main Campus where Snidecor Hall is now located. These operated until the turn of the century when they were abandoned as both unsafe and unprofitable. The land was then rented to farmers, but they had little success due to the land's poor-quality topsoil and lack of adequate water.

In 1913, most of the Den land passed into the hands of speculators Jack and Coto Cavalleto, who purchased 200 acres on the eastern end with a $5,000 down payment. In 1920, Jack Cavaletto sold his 99 acres to Col. Colin Campbell for about $65,000, while Coto sold his to other speculators for $52,000. Ruins of the Campbell estate can still be found just west of the Devereux Slough and portions of the estate's bathhouse remain on the beach just east of Coal Oil Point. Eventually, the Devereux Foundation, a private school for slow-learning and emotionally disturbed children, purchased the Campbell property for $100,000.

During the 1920s, what was still an unnamed, mostly uninhabited mesa was subdivided with the intention of turning it into a resort community. This was never a very successful project, perhaps because of the abundance of tar on the beach.

During that period, three subdivisions were created but without coordination. This resulted in the present nonalignment of east-west streets that is apparent along Camino Corto and Camino Pescadero. One of the street-namers of the period didn't know the Spanish language very well, resulting in "Del Playa," instead of "De la Playa." However, the largest of these subdivisions was called "Isla Vista" -- literally "island view" -- and the name stuck for the entire area.

After the resort fantasy petered out, the Signal Oil Co. purchased most of Isla Vista when oil was discovered west of I.V. in 1928. This also was not a very successful project, and, except for a couple of dozen beach houses and a few cows and goats, Isla Vista was pretty much uninhabited at the outbreak of World War II.

Setting the Stage

During World War II, the Santa Barbara airport and what is now the UCSB Main Campus were a Marine Air Base. At the end of one of John Wayne's WW II movies, he says that he is returning from the Pacific arena to the Marine base at Goleta. During the war, a Japanese submarine actually torpedoed the coastline just west of Isla Vista, the only strike against U.S. soil during the war. One

Adventurer George Fremont brought his band over San Marcos Pass in 1846, effectively ending the Mexican Territory Period. Although California soon joined the United States, land holdings from the Mexican era were maintained. This is a detail of the Dan Sayre Groesbeck mural in the Santa Barbara County Courthouse.

story has it, however, that this was not an intentional strike against the U.S. mainland, but an attempt by one submarine commander to gain some revenge for an insult he received while laboring here as a farmworker some years earlier.

After the war, the Marines sold the portion of the Isla Vista mesa they owned to the Regents of the University of California for the nominal amount of $10. In 1953, the 1,725-student campus of Santa Barbara College moved from its columned-campus in the foothills above Santa Barbara (now the site of Brooks Institute of Photography) to what is now the UCSB Main Campus. Santa Barbara College, a teachers college formed initially in the Twenties, became a campus in the UC system shortly before the move. The siting of the UCSB campus on the Isla Vista mesa turned out to be a windfall for two area landowners who joined the UC Regents a few years later.

Because oil production in Isla Vista never paid off, Signal Oil was stuck with nearly worthless land. But Samuel Mosher, the president of Signal Oil, was appointed to the UC Board of Regents in 1954, serving until 1967.

During this period, the UC Regents decided to leave the half-square-mile residential section of the new UCSB campus (that is, Isla Vista) for private development, instead of buying it and building a university community of dorms and apartment complexes. This

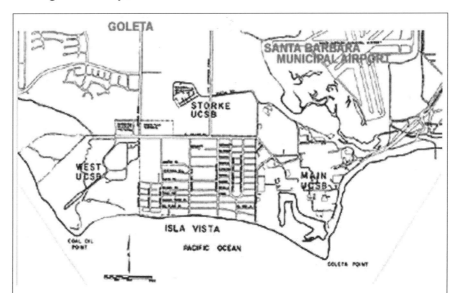

Isla Vista is 0.55 square miles, excluding the UCSB campus, which now includes Francisco Torres Residence Hall. The City of Goleta lies to the north and west, while the Santa Barbara Municipal Airport lies to the northeast, adjacent to UCSB's Main Campus. Map from Recommendations for Isla Vista Planning (1973).

significantly increased the value of all properties in Isla Vista.

In 1955, another local businessman, Thomas Storke, was also appointed to the UC Regents. He served until 1960. Storke owned the Santa Barbara *News-Press*, the region's major daily newspaper. He also owned 89 acres adjacent to the new UCSB campus, stretching north from El Colegio Road to Hollister Avenue and what would become Storke Road.

Sometime in this period the Regents raised the planned enrollment for UCSB from 10,000 to 25,000 (it then had roughly 2,500 students), providing a further stimulus to property values in and around Isla Vista. To accommodate this development, the University purchased a big chunk of Storke's property for $1.15 million. After Storke kicked back half of this prize as a contribution to the University, UCSB named the property, a bell tower, a building, and a major academic achievement award in his honor.

The announcement that UCSB intended to increase its enrollment ten-fold touched off a building boom in Isla Vista and throughout the Goleta Valley. Since it was estimated that four additional people came to the area for each new student, it was obvious that there was a lot of profit to be made in housing development. But money was needed to make this happen, and for this the Goleta Valley Savings & Loan was formed in 1962 -- the same year that Vernon Cheadle became chancellor at UCSB.

Samuel Mosher

Samuel Mosher was a graduate of UC Berkeley where he majored in agriculture. He was founder and owner of Signal Oil Company. However, orchid growing became his avocation and he founded Dos Pueblos Orchid Company in Goleta to pursue that interest. During World War II he was a director of the National Petroleum War Council. After the war, he was a founder and chairman of the board of the Flying Tiger Line.

In 1967, Mosher contributed UCSB's first major unrestricted gift ($93,937) and that followed a $100,000 gift in 1965 toward the building of the University Center (completed in 1966). By 1995, the Mosher Foundation had contributed over $2.1 million to UCSB for scholarships, athletics, buildings, and general use.

Mosher also made a significant donation to help build the University Religious Center in Isla Vista and the auditorium there was named in his honor in 1971.

Source: UCSB Alumni Association.

Thomas Storke

Thomas Storke was born in Santa Barbara, Calif., November 23, 1876; graduated from Stanford University, Palo Alto, Calif., 1898; editor and publisher of the Santa Barbara *News-Press* and its predecessors; rancher and citrus fruit grower; postmaster, Santa Barbara 1914-1921; appointed on Nov. 9, 1938, as a Democrat to the United States Senate to fill the vacancy caused by the resignation of William Gibbs McAdoo and served to January 3, 1939; was not a candidate for election for the full term; resumed newspaper business; member of the board of regents of University of California 1955-1960; died in Santa Barbara, Oct. 12, 1971.

Source: http://bioguide.congress.gov/scripts/biodisplay.pl?index=S000973

Editor and publisher of the local daily newspaper, Thomas Storke was also a UC Regent who owned 89 acres contiguous on the north to the new UCSB campus.

To accommodate an inflated long-term enrollment goal of 25,000 set by the UC Regents during his tenure (even the Long Range Development Plan for UCSB under discussion in 2008 calls only has an eventual enrollment of 25,000 by the year 2025), the university purchased a big chunk of Storke's property for $1.15 million.

After Storke donated back half of this money to the university, UCSB named the property, the above-pictured bell tower, the building that it rises from, the plaza it is on, and a major academic achievement award in his honor.

Isla Vista *Free Press* photograph.

The 1960s Building Boom

The Goleta Valley Savings & Loan was a most unusual financial institution. According to research published in 1969 by the investigative Isla Vista newspaper *Probe*, the Goleta Valley S&L completely turned around the national lending average. While the typical S&L lent 15% of its capital to developers, this one lent 85%. Also interesting is a partial list of the board of directors of this S&L:

Vernon Cheadle, UCSB Chancellor (1962-76) pointing at an aerial photograph of Isla Vista. Isla Vista Slide Show photograph.

    * Samuel Mosher, UC Regent and Signal Oil president

    * Daniel Frost, Mosher's attorney and also a Signal Oil director

    * John Harlen, local developer and Signal Oil's property manager in Isla Vista

    * Thomas Storke, former UC Regent, publisher of the area's daily newspaper, and the owner of significant property adjacent to the campus

    * Bert Lare, Storke's general manager

    * Vernon Cheadle, the new chancellor at UCSB

By the mid-'60s the property moguls were getting ready to create the modern Isla Vista, and the UCSB Administration, a power bloc in its own right, seemed to be helping out.

The Role of the County

In order to fully capitalize on the profit potential of this opportunity, a plan was hatched to zone Isla Vista for maximum occupancy. This is where the Santa Barbara County Board of Supervisors came into play. Today, the highest-price apartments in Isla Vista are along Del Playa Drive and they are packed like sardines in a can. Although they have little off-street parking, they are built right up to the edge of the bluff, leaving owners begging to build seawalls in recent years. Some buildings have even had to be condemned and moved off the eroding bluffs. Even inland, there are a lot more cars than parking places and several areas have densities unmatched in the state. In fact, it has been estimated that Isla Vista's half-square-mile residential section is the most densely populated community west of the Mississippi

River. A 1970 issue of *Probe* explains how this happened.

In the early 1960s, the Board of Supervisors formed a committee to "investigate" zoning for Isla Vista. The committee was made up of John Harlen, Signal Oil's I.V. property manager, Jack Schwartz, an I.V. realtor, and Carl Chandler, an Isla Vista property owner and the assistant to Dan Grant, the County supervisor for Isla Vista and Goleta.

What this committee came up with was a custom-made plan, unique in the state, called "Student-Residential" zoning. An "S" prefix on regular R-2 (duplexes) or R-4 (multi-story apartments) zoning meant that such areas did not have to conform to the usual minimum set backs from either the street or bluff, did not have to have the usual number of parking spaces per bedroom, etc., etc.

The "S" designation also promoted the combination of lots to enable construction of larger apartment buildings than would have been allowed in other parts of the county.

BEFORE and AFTER: Isla Vista in 1963 (above) and Isla Vista in 1970 (below).

Many people protested this plan, but the Board of Supervisors listened only to what they wanted to hear. In Schwartz's now infamous speech before the Board of Supervisors in favor of the "SR" zoning plan, he stated: "These kids arrive here with a sleeping bag and a surf board." The Isla Vista we have come to know was thrown together in the next few years -- 33% paved over and 96% renters.

At the same time, the entire Goleta Valley, including Isla Vista, grew from 19,000 residents in 1960 to 69,000 in 1970.

The 6600 block of Del Playa Drive in 1988. Isla Vista *Free Press* photo.

The Role of the University

During this era of Isla Vista's rapid development, the UCSB Administration was not aggressively acting to create decent living conditions for its students, faculty, and staff, either on campus or in the area located entirely within the campus boundaries (Isla Vista) that the Regents had decided to leave for private development. Perhaps this was not entirely the fault of local UC officials, because there was a lot of pressure being applied from the statewide UC system. Indeed, at the request of some Goleta Valley developers, the UC Regents at one point ordered the halt of any new housing developments on campus for several years.

Still, an independent report requested by the UC Regents, which attempted to understand the causes of the 1970 civil disturbances in Isla Vista, stated clearly that the UCSB Administration "failed to protect the orderly development of a university community in Isla Vista." (The Trow Report,

Even six blocks inland, the 6600 block of Picasso Rd., is just as crowded.

1970). See Chapter 3.

Given the intertwining of public and private interests that apparently occurred, this conclusion is probably not too surprising.

. . . an independent report requested by the UC Regents, which attempted to understand the causes of the 1970 civil disturbances in Isla Vista, stated clearly that the UCSB Administration "failed to protect the orderly development of a university community in Isla Vista."

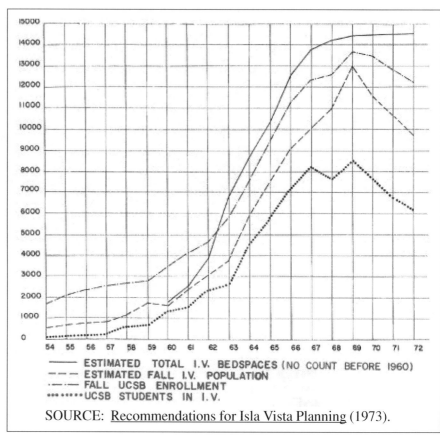

SOURCE: <u>Recommendations for Isla Vista Planning</u> (1973).

This chapter is an adaptation of JoAnne Yokota's "A Short History of Isla Vista" (1971) and Abbie Haight's "A Tragicall Historie of Isla Vista" (1972), both published by the Isla Vista Community Council.

CHAPTER 2
THE CIVIL DISTURBANCES OF 1969-70

by Malcolm Gault-Williams

At the end of the 1960s, Isla Vista was much more than its physical setting – it was one of hundreds of college towns across America caught up in a cultural insurgency. The Vietnam War and the military draft that sustained it impacted all youth, as did the sexual revolution, the widespread use of marijuana and psychedelic drugs and popular music that openly urged rebellion against the "system." But Isla Vista's physical setting, so cynically thrown together by local political and propertied interests, provided for a particularly intense combination of these ingredients and, in retrospect, was widely viewed as the fundamental cause of why things got so out of hand.

"The idea of this prosecution [in Chicago] was to chill all of us . . . to set an example to show you what could happen if you became involved in any social movement -- to put fear where fervor was and destroy fervor, to destroy involvement. No trial should take place in the United States that embodies a threat to the soul of mankind."

"Chicago 8" Attorney William Kunstler speaking at UCSB's Harder Stadium
February 25, 1970
Photograph from the movie, "Don't Bank on Amerika" (1970)

On February 24, 1970 local activists Lefty Bryant, Greg Wilkinson, Jim Trotter, and Mick Kronman were arrested on trumped-up charges against Lefty, then a black student leader. That night, in response, between 150 and 200 people gathered in the loop area of Isla Vista, setting fires in trash cans, vandalizing some realty offices (the town was, and remains, 96% renters), and breaking a window at the Isla Vista branch of the Bank of America.

Local Issues: In 1968, the Black Students' Union (BSU) took over the UCSB Computer Science Building in a demand for a Black Studies curriculum. Because this was a similar demand being made at campuses across the country, the University eventually consented. But arresting black student activists on unusual charges became a common event.

At the right is a picture of BSU activist Rahidi Ali being arrested on the street in Isla Vista for reportedly not paying his rent on time. Photograph from the Isla Vista Slide Show.

The next afternoon, civil rights attorney William Kunstler spoke before about 3,000 people in Harder Stadium on the UCSB campus. Kunstler talked mostly about the trial of the "Chicago 8" that was in progress and for which he was the lead attorney. The trial concerned eight anti-war activists -- including Tom Hayden, Abbie Hoffman, Jerry Rubin, Dave Dillenger, and Bobby Seale -- who were accused of interrupting the 1968 Democratic Convention. However, Kunstler related local issues and instances of similar government and police attempts to squelch the student anti-war/counter-culture movement across the country by arresting its leaders.

Local Issues: The summer of 1969 saw the infamous oil spill from an offshore drilling rig, which covered Santa Barbara's beaches and launched the environmental movement nationally.

Local Issues: That fall, there was a successful campaign to block a plan to build a highway along the northern perimeter of the UCSB campus through the Goleta Slough.

Kunstler had addressed perhaps 3,000 people in Harder Stadium in the late afternoon of February 25. Following his speech, many people walked back toward the center of Isla Vista. Numerous police units

Local Issues: In the fall of 1969, a popular anti-war instructor in the Anthropology Department, Bill Allen, was denied tenure and 7,776 students signed a petition demanding an open review of the decision. Demonstrations in front of the UCSB Administration Building became almost a daily event and were often dispersed by police. Allen was fired without the required hearing. Photograph of Allen speaking in front of the UCSB Administration Building is from the I.V. Slide Show.

were patrolling Isla Vista in what was called a "saturation patrol technique." Suddenly, police singled out Rich Underwood, another student leader who had figured prominently in the Bill Allen demonstrations,

charged him with carrying a molotov cocktail (it was actually an open bottle of wine), and began beating him up on the spot.

Police then began swinging their clubs at people almost at random as they walked back into Isla Vista from the stadium. However, dozens of people began pushing back and soon hundreds more joined them in the center of town.

"It was this incident, one more incident of wanton police harassment, which the people in Isla Vista -- the students -- said: 'I've had enough!',", recalled Greg Knell, then vice president of the UCSB Associated Students. "This is our community, and this occupying army must be driven out."

As people walked back into town following William Kunstler's speech at Harder Stadium, police began beating up people almost at random. Photograph from the movie, Don't Bank on Amerika.

Shortly before midnight on Feb. 25, 1970, the Isla Vista branch of the Bank of America was broken into and a fire started by persons still unknown. Hundreds gathered to watch the blaze. Photograph from the Isla Vista Slide Show.

The battle raged for hours. Police cars were set on fire, attacks were mounted on the Bank of America, and several waves of police forces were beaten back by street-fighting Isla Vistans.

"All of a sudden, all you heard out of the windows was the Rolling Stones' 'Street Fighting Man,'" said one student later. "I was amazed at the fury that people showed that night," another participant said. "People charging like gladiators with trash lids as shields, throwing rocks at the cops . . . . You saw people walking around with a light in their eyes and a look on their face that you just never experienced in everyday life."

Far outnumbered, the police finally retreated out of town.

"There were hours at a time when there was nothing to do but enjoy being in liberated territory," one person said.

In this power vacuum people began seriously trashing the offices of the local rental agencies.

Toward midnight, people who are still unidentified, broke down the front doors of the bank and successfully lit a fire inside. Bank records served as kindling. Hundreds of people participated

The Isla Vista branch of the Bank of America on the morning of February 26, 1970. Photograph from the Isla Vista Slide Show.

in one way or another, then watched it burn through the night. By dawn, the building was a smoldering ruin and Isla Vista had become national news.

The first Isla Vista riot — I.V. I as it later became known — ended several days later when then-Governor Ronald Reagan sent in the National Guard to militarily occupy the town.

Music of the Times

Ohio by Neil Young

Tin soldiers and Nixon coming
We're finally on our own.
This summer I hear the
    drumming,
Four dead in Ohio.

Got to get down to it

Soldiers are gunning us down.
Should have been done long ago.

What if you knew her
And found her dead on the ground?
How can you run when you know?

Subsequent riots I.V. II and I.V. III attempted in different ways to recreate that incredible feeling of liberation. These efforts exacted a heavy price.

Isla Vista II

In early April, after Yippee leader Jerry Rubin was prohibited from speaking in Santa Barbara County, I.V. II broke out. During the civil disobedience aimed at the reopened bank, dump trucks filled with police circled the downtown area. Suddenly, there was a gun shot and UCSB student Kevin Patrick Moran, who was on the front steps of the bank trying to put out a fire, was killed.

A reporter in the field that night from the student radio station KCSB-FM, filed a report both chilling and graphic:

"We have what could be termed an extremely tense and extremely frightening situation. Because you see shadows of police lurking in the dark and you hear rifles cocking in the background."

UCSB student Kevin P. Moran was shot and killed by a policeman ironically while trying to put out a fire on the steps of the rebuilt Bank of America on April 18, 1970. Isla Vista Slide Show photo. When the bank reopened, the plaque pictured below was embedded at the entrance to the building. Isla Vista *Free Press* photo. The bank closed this branch in 1981, replacing it with an ATM down the block. Today the building is UCSB's Embarcadero Lecture Hall.

Sheriff Captain Joel Honey, caught here on camera by *Time* magazine with his medieval mace and sword, was in charge of local police during I.V. II.

For days the Sheriff's Department claimed that a sniper had killed Moran, even issuing a description of the shooter. A court inquiry subsequently ruled that Moran had been killed by an "accidental" discharge from the gun of a City of Santa Barbara police officer, David Gosselin, from a dump truck. Gosselin went free.

FOR SOCIAL CHANGE FAIR PLAY AND PEACE KEVIN P. MORAN APRIL 18, 1970

After reporting this and other events in a play-by-play mode, KCSB was shut down the morning after Moran's death by local law enforcement and UCSB officials. This action was obviously in violation of federal law.

Kent State

After I.V. II, there was a feeling of "Who would die next." President Richard Nixon's unconstitutional bombing of Cambodia and the killing of four students at Kent State University in Ohio by the National Guard came just a few weeks later.

At this time, UCSB Vice Chancellor Stephen Goodspeed said publicly that he felt "there were 100 hard-core revolutionaries in Isla Vista and 400 or 500 leftists who sided with the revolutionaries. There were also 4,000 or 5,000 moderates who can swing either way, and swung left during I.V. I, and 4,000 or 5,000 who are apathetic."

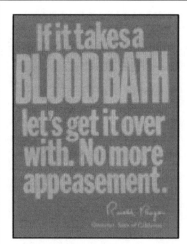

A poster quoting then-Gov. Ronald Reagan's succinct understanding of the times.

Isla Vista III

I.V. III began when indictments were handed down in early June to those who had supposedly burned the bank. True to form and very similar to Kunstler's description of how the Chicago 8 had been picked to be prosecuted, the Santa Barbara 17 appeared to be a list of the most outspoken and effective student and community leaders, rather than a group that actually might have been responsible for the fire. In fact, two of the 17 had been in jail the night the bank was burned.

The indictments kindled widespread resentment in Isla Vista. They were introduced into a climate already very sensitive to possible judicial abuses. Robert Potter and James J. Sullivan in their booklet said of the indictments that:

"The timing was also unfortunate, many students felt, because the trial seemed deliberately planned to be held after most students had left the area for the summer. [Additionally] the Bank of America's earlier offer of large rewards was felt by many to have probably produced false information. Even the least radical of Isla Vista's population angrily felt that the beleaguered

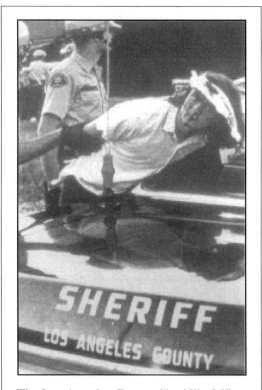

The Los Angeles County Sheriff's Office was part of the military occupation of Isla Vista for several weeks in the spring of 1970. Isla Vista Slide Show photograph.

community did not need this further difficulty, especially at a time when recently established projects were promising real success with Isla Vista's problems." p. 98

The major recently established project was the birth of the Isla Vista Community Council (IVCC) in May, which for the first time gave Isla Vistans at least an advisory vote in local governmental decisions. Eighteen-year-olds didn't begin voting until 1972, but any resident at least 16 was permitted to vote in IVCC elections.

The Isla Vista Community Federal Credit Union also opened its doors that spring, which had a bail fund for those arrested in town.

A sign painted on the Phi Sigma Kappa fraternity house urging the Los Angeles Sheriff's Office to end its brutal occupation of Isla Vista during the spring of 1970. Isla Vista Slide Show photograph.

Perfect Park

So many people were fed up with these legal tactics and the continued occupation of Isla Vista that a massive sit-in at Isla Vista's Perfect Park was called to protest the right to peaceful demonstration. Perfect Park was a large, undeveloped parcel of land at the top of the Loop where Embarcadero del Mar meets Embarcadero del Norte. It had been a major gathering place for several years, hosting live bands and anti-war speeches on most weekends. However, this property was privately owned by a Santa Monica physician, who seldom visited it and seldom protested its unofficial status as the primary gathering place in downtown Isla Vista.

On June 10, 1970, over 1,000 people -- UCSB students and faculty, local residents, and area clergy -- participated in a sit-in at Perfect Park in intentional violation of a curfew issued by the sheriff. Police charged near sunset, teargassing most people off the property, but many were dragged off and arrested. The police then expanded their operations from the downtown area into the residential portions of Isla Vista. At the end of the day, 390 people had been arrested and carted off to the County jail.

It was such an egregious act that Joseph Lodge, the Municipal Court Judge reviewing the case, released all those arrested the following morning.

Years later, speaking in Isla Vista at an event held in conjunction with the 30th anniversary of the bank burning, Judge Lodge said: "At the time, with everything going on nationally and locally, I thought we could be at the beginning of a civil war, and by releasing the demonstrators I was picking sides."

Furthermore, at the judge's retirement party in 2003, four out of the six speakers eulogizing him – all long-standing attorneys in Santa Barbara — mentioned that his freeing of the Isla Vista protestors back in 1970 was what they most admired about his career.

There had been cases of police abuse in the previous riots, but during I.V. III, police misconduct really became an issue due to the overzealous actions of the Los Angeles Special Tactical Squad and other police.

The Delta Omega fraternity's president stated: "The use of force was just totally got out of hand. The students — even people like me — started to get a little hot about the approach that was taken."

One of those indicted, Walt Chesnavich, said: "Every day I would hear stories about what the L.A. Tactical Squad was doing the night

One of the 1,000 non-violent demonstrators in Isla Vista's Perfect Park being hauled off to jail on June 10, 1970. This Isla Vista Slide Show photograph was later used in a campaign to raise money to build the monument in Perfect Park to the anti-war movement around the world.

I knew of people that were thrown off roofs, people that had to be hospitalized . . . the police came in . . . they'd march down the street, just hundreds of 'em, 40-at-a-time . . . . It was war, that's basically what it was. It was our community against the police.

CHRIS ATTWOOD
UCSB student

before, kicking down doors and dragging people around . . . . If the things they said about police brutality weren't true before the L.A. police came, it sure as hell was true after they came; it created its own riot."

As Chris Attwood, a student who later became a leader in the effort to build a new community in Isla Vista in the early 1970s, put it: "I knew of people that were thrown off roofs, people that had to be hospitalized . . . the police came in . . . we couldn't leave our homes (due to the curfew) . . . they gassed our homes . . . . You know, they'd march down the street, just hundreds of 'em, 40-at-a-time . . . . It was war, that's basically what it was. It was our community against the police. What it did for this town, I think at least for several years, was one of the most incredible things I've ever seen. During this time, people were on the streets. Everyone had to depend on everyone else. There wasn't any other way to survive."

Isla Vista III's Final Toll

The Santa Barbara Citizens Commission on Civil Disorders convened later in June to examine the events of that winter and spring.

The final report stated that The Faculty-Clergy Observer Program group turned over to the Attorney General's office and the FBI over 300 signed complaints against law enforcement officers for the period June 6th to 12th, alleging:

* 113 persons beaten
* 60 dwellings illegally entered and searched
* 48 instances of willful destruction of personal property
* 34 persons arrested on private property for curfew violations
* 6 instances of improper familiarities with arrested women
* a long list of alleged brutalities en route to the jail and in the jail

This chapter is based on an article written by Malcolm Gault-Williams for the Isla Vista Free Press in 1987. Gault-Williams is the author of the book Don't Bank on Amerika: the History of the Isla Vista Riots of 1970. Read more about it at www.legendarysurfers.com.

Gault-Williams lived in Isla Vista in 1970, moved away shortly afterwards and returned in 1983. He was the station manager at the UCSB campus radio station KCSB-FM from 1984 to 1989 and was elected to the Isla Vista Park Board during that period. He currently lives in Santa Barbara and works at the UCSB Library.

Malcolm Gault-Williams
I.V. *Free Press* photo, 1987.

CHAPTER 3
THE AFTERMATH

<u>Analysis and Restrospective: An Interview with Dick Flacks</u>

Richard Flacks was a founding member of the radical student group Students for a Democratic Society (SDS) while an undergraduate at the University of Michigan. He taught sociology at UCSB from 1969 through 2004 and was one of the university's most popular professors.

One of his specialties was the "youth culture" of the 1960s and 1970s, of which Isla Vista is a famous example. In his Social Movements class, he always shows the movie "Don't Bank on Amerika," a history of the civil disturbances in Isla Vista during the spring of 1970. He also often puts together a panel discussion among people who were involved in those 1970 activities.

Flacks wrote a book with Jack Whalen entitled <u>Echoes of Rebellion</u> based on interviews with student activists in Isla Vista and on campus in

Dick Flacks. I.V. *Free Press* photo, 1988.

1970. The Temple University Press published the book in 1989; the University of California Press declined to print it.

I conducted this interview, which was first published in the Isla Vista Free Press *in 1988. -- C.L.*

FREE PRESS: What I remember most from one of those panel discussions I attended was the statement by several of the panelists that in Isla Vista in 1970, that everyone felt that all of the issues were related. That is, if your landlord screwed you over, it reinforced your opposition to the Vietnam War or your anger with your parents. Could you explain this further for us?

FLACKS: If you think, as most of the activists did, that we live in a "system" and it's a unified system of domination, then what happened to you with your landlord in I.V. or with the police in I.V. was akin to what was happening in Vietnam, etc.

FREE PRESS: Was there anything really unique about Isla Vista, as distinct from what was going on in other college communities across the nation?

FLACKS: What struck me very strongly when I arrived here from the University of Chicago was that there was a much more pervasive and

Social systems of control are pretty fragile to begin with. And when they got challenged in a very comprehensive way, they collapsed.

DICK FLACKS

integrated sense of rebellion against authority here. And this wasn't just among the activists! I mean, your father was a part of it, the police was a part of it, the University Administration was a part of it. Nixon was part of it.

In a sense, everyone in their youth rebels against authority. But you learn to suppress and control these feelings because these feelings are unsafe, even dangerous. So, you learn to "play by the rules," at least outwardly. Maybe you'll break some of the rules in private; that kind of split of the "self" is quite ordinary.

But, what happened here was that there was some kind of mass release from that need to suppress the rebellion. When thousands of people are marching in defiance of authority, suddenly you become "authorized" to rebel against that authority, to express those buried feelings. And, there was an emotional, psychological release in expressing them, especially with a whole lot of other people expressing them, too.

Social systems of control are pretty fragile to begin with. And when they got challenged in a very comprehensive way, they collapsed.

FREE PRESS: What were the major contributing factors to this "rebellion" in Isla Vista that year?

FLACKS: There were several factors of many people's everyday experiences that led to this collapse, or at least reinforced it:

1. The drug scene. People were involved with various kinds of drugs (marijuana, LSD, etc.), and these were all illegal. And it is revealed to you that the very practice of these very pleasurable activities is all tied up with being an outlaw.

2. Movies in I.V. The movies at the Magic Lantern Theater in I.V. that fall and spring included "Z" [the story of a wonderfully honest, idealistic politician in Greece who was assassinated], "Easy Rider" [two guys on the road who get wiped out by some red necks], "Alice's Restaurant" [about a hippy commune that gets smashed by the forces of darkness], "Medium Cool" [about some people who get caught up in the demonstrations at the Democratic Convention in Chicago and get killed], "The Baffle of Algiers" [which implied that revolutionary violence was justified]. These were all powerful and had a big impact.

3. The Bill Allen Incident. A popular anthropology professor was fired and a lot of students thought it was because he talked about Vietnam in his classes. This provoked major demonstrations on campus with 7,776 people signing a petition asking for an open hearing on his firing, supposedly required by UCSB guidelines.

4. Ronald Reagan was governor at that time and both his language and actions were very repressive.

Anthropology Instructor Bill Allen was fired without the required review hearing despite a petition signed by 7,776 UCSB students. Here he's being interviewed by the media in 1970. Isla Vista Slide Show photograph.

5. The police repression in Isla Vista, which so many people had experienced first hand.

6. The Generation Gap in values between these activists and their parents.

7. The oil spill in Santa Barbara the year before.

There was also a lot of popular music at the time that shouted out for rebellion. For example:

Almost Cut My Hair & **Ohio**: Crosby, Stills Nash & Young.

White Rabbit & **Volunteers**: Jefferson Airplane

Street Fighting Man: The Rolling Stones

Masters of War & **Times They Are a Changin'**: Bob Dylan

-- *C.L.*

8. The draft of young people to serve in an unpopular war was accompanied by a general collapse of authority nationwide, especially with Nixon's presidency. I mean, this wasn't a war supported by a widespread, patriotic movement.

So, when these common experiences were combined with such deep-felt needs to express rebellion against illegitimate authority, this all got released in mass demonstrations.

I suppose, too, that the close proximity of so many people of the same age [*Free Press:* 75% of I.V. residents at that time were UCSB students -- it's been about 60% since 1990, up from 50% in the mid-

'70s] in such a densely packed, ghetto environment, added a lot to this common experience.

This was the biggest difference between what I saw here and what was happening in the East, where it was primarily political activists who were at the forefront of the demonstrations. But here, it was a much broader spectrum of people who were involved, and they were involved more to release cultural repression than just to achieve political goals.

In other words, it was the golden sons and daughters of California who burned down the Bank of America. This was a new generation of people who were convinced that the values their parents were trying to teach them just didn't work -- because they weren't working in the parents' lives.

What Whalen and I discovered in interviewing a lot of the I.V. activists of that time was they were overwhelmed with the feeling that there was some kind of Apocalypse coming. There was a pervasive belief that everything was coming to a head, and that there was no sense in planning for the future, at least in a personal sense, because the U.S. was headed toward some kind of civil war, some kind of total conflict.

The things which were going on in I.V. were also happening across the country. For example, the killing of four people by the National Guard at Kent State University.

I believe, too, that if these same people came through Isla Vista five years earlier, they wouldn't have been involved in these activities. But, it was this amazing combination of personal and social experiences which lead to the events we are recalling.

FREE PRESS: So, what has happened to the people who burned down the Bank of America and the leaders in Isla Vista during the winter and spring of 1970?

> *(W)hen these common experiences were combined with such deep-felt needs to express rebellion against illegitimate authority, this all got released in mass demonstrations.*
>
> *I suppose, too, that the close proximity of so many people of the same age in such a densely packed, ghetto environment, added a lot to this common experience.*
>
> *In other words, it was the golden sons and daughters of California who burned down the Bank of America. This was a new generation of people who were convinced that the values their parents were trying to teach them just didn't work -- because they weren't working in the parents' lives.*
>
> DICK FLACKS

FLACKS: For, the most part, these activists have spent 15 years searching for a niche or role in society, experimenting with many different life styles and occupational pathways. And, these people are not, for the most part, doing what they were trained for in college. And, their income per year is not impressive.

But, the group we followed in the study who were not involved in the demonstrations, a lot of fraternity and sorority people and athletes -- the so-called "straights" of the time -- who were angry about the police brutality but who did not identify with the rebellion of that winter and spring, these people are for the most part still involved with the same occupational field they chose coming out of college and their earnings are in the six figures. And, most got married and settled down right away.

That's why the movie, "The Big Chill," was such a distortion, because it purports to tell the story of people who were activists in the '60s and '70s, now turning into Yuppies. In fact, this movie told the story of the so-called "straight" people of that era. The story of the generation that made the events in Isla Vista has yet to be told.

Isla Vista POW. A popular graduation "gown" that June of 1970. Photo from the movie "Don't Bank on Amerika" (1970).

FREE PRESS: So what happened after that spring? I mean, what happened the next fall in Isla Vista?

FLACKS: The most amazing thing! The Apocalypse didn't happen. The activists started building a community. There was a general coming together of people to create some order in the chaos.

Not some kind of order imposed from outside, but an order based on self-improvement.

I really learned a lot from that experience. It seems that when people get close to the edge, most of them draw back and ask, "Can we make something of what's here?"

Even that spring, some of this started when the Isla Vista Community Council was established. Then came Regents funds in the fall and a whole group of community institutions were established, all on so-called "alternative" models -- organizations which hopefully reflected the new values being expressed by this new generation. See Chapter 4.

Of course, the rest is history.

The panel discussion among Isla Vista activists of the 1970-era that occurred February 15, 1988 included (from left to right) UCSB Sociology Professor Dick Flacks, Castilo de la Rocha, Bob Langfelder, Becca Wilson, Joann Frankfort, and Mitch Kronman. Isla Vista *Free Press* photo.

Five Activists Look Back on the Events of 1970

On February 15th, 1988, several Isla Vista activists from the 1970 era gathered to discuss their experiences in the studio of KCTY, community television in Santa Barbara. UCSB Sociology Professor Dick Flacks was the moderator of the panel. I made the excerpts that follow. -- C.L.

WHERE WERE YOU WHILE THE BANK OF AMERICA WAS BURNING?

Langfelder: I was out in front with hundreds of other people watching it. I remember that we got a few beers from the takeout across the street, which was doing a great business!

Kronman: I was in jail.

Wilson: I was at the offices of the *Gaucho*, the name of the student newspaper at the time.

WHY WAS THE BANK BURNED?

Langfelder: The B of A was the most convenient symbol of authority. Plus, it was a central building in I.V., yet isolated enough from the rest of town that a fire there wouldn't spread.

de la Rocha: Plus, the *Gaucho* had been running stories about the role of the Bank in the farming

31

industry in California and the tie to pesticides, which where harmful to farmworkers, plus the Bank's role in financing the Vietnam War. At the time, A.S. [the UCSB Associated Students Legislative Council] was debating taking their money out of the bank, too.

Langfelder: There had been several days of throwing rocks at the bank, but there had been no planning of sabotage; the actual burning of the bank was a completely spontaneous act. It was after Kunstler's speech in Harder Stadium that day that the crowd's mood changed a lot -- they were much more willing to take risks in their challenge.

de la Rocha: It's important to understand that only the bank and the real estate companies were trashed during that time; the targets

WHAT LED UP TO THE BANK BEING BURNED AND THE OTHER PROTESTS?

Kronman: A lot of things came together. I think that it was the Black Student's Union takeover of North Hall in 1968 that really started it off, locally at least. This galvanized a lot of people, woke them up.

> WHAT LED UP TO THE
> BANK BEING BURNED AND
> THE OTHER PROTESTS?
>
> *I think that it was the Black Student's Union takeover of North Hall in 1968 that really started it off, locally at least. This galvanized a lot of people, woke them up.*
>
> MITCH KRONMAN

Wilson: We were all really impressed with the boldness of that action — it was an example to all of us of commitment that took risks. But a month before the Bank went down, 3-4,000 people had been gathered peacefully, and politely, in front of the UCSB Administration Building to protest the firing of Bill Allen without the required open hearing. We had the petition signed by 7,776 people in favor of the hearing.

And they called in the police to remove us! And the police beat up a lot of us. It was a shock to all of us, both that the Administration was completely unwilling to negotiate and that they would order police to come onto campus to remove us.

Plus, there had been months of police harassment and brutality in I.V.

> *. . . a month before the Bank went down, 3-4,000 people had been gathered peacefully, and politely, in front of the UCSB Administration Building to protest the firing of Bill Allen without the required open hearing. We had the petition signed by 7,776 people in favor of the hearing. And they called in the police to remove us! And the police beat up a lot of us. It was a shock to all of us, both that the Administration was completely unwilling to negotiate and that they would order police to come onto campus to remove us. Plus, there had been months of police harassment and brutality in I.V.*
>
> BECCA WILSON

de la Rocha: But behind all of this was the war in Vietnam. The war was the real unifying force among a lot of divergent groups. The activism of the Black Student Union demonstrated the common bonds between all of these groups.

Kronman: Plus, you can't leave out the cultural revolution, which was sweeping the country at that time. It was the music, drugs, the into-the-streets culture, the throwing off of old ways such as the challenging of sexism and racism. All of this was being-covered by the national media, and it wasn't lost on us that we were part of a much bigger phenomena.

> *We were intoxicated with a sense that there was going to be a revolution not any further away than two years. There was a mood of great change expected sweeping across the land, and we felt that these changes would have tremendous long-term impacts on the way everyone lived.*
>
> JOANN FRANKFORT

Langfelder: While this may have been the only bank to be burned to the ground, a lot of banks across the U.S. were being trashed, and people were being killed by authorities in a lot of places.

WHAT WAS YOUR VISION OF THE FUTURE AT THAT TIME?

Frankfort: We were intoxicated with a sense that there was going to be a revolution not any further away than two years. There was a mood of great change sweeping across the land, and we felt that these changes would have tremendous long-term impacts on the way everyone lived.

Langfelder: We thought that people should put their personal career-development plans on hold and to dedicate themselves to this big change: If we could push it over the top, everything else would work out.

Frankfort: We had a political vision of the future, not a personal one. We were all welded into what we thought was a very large movement and we weren't thinking about personal goals such as jobs, homes, new cars, etc.

WHAT HAPPENED AFTER THE BANK EVENT?

Langfelder: During the 5-6 hours that the police had been chased out of town, there was this great feeling of exhilaration; we had liberated Isla Vista. But things soon changed as the police came back in force and reoccupied the town for several months.

Frankfort: A police helicopter actually landed on the roof of my apartment. I don't think that I will ever forget the horror of that feeling. After Kevin Moran was killed, it really began to sink into me how real, and how depressing all of this was.

de la Rocha: After the re-occupation, it became difficult to meet — any of our groups — because we were so concerned about being infiltrated by the F.B.I., etc. Everyone got real paranoid. The tremendous repression changed all of the optimism we had before.

Wilson: We were all afraid of being rounded up. Instead of a great revolution, we felt like the U.S. was headed toward a fascist state. The tremendous optimism we felt before changed to depression. People started buying guns, a lot of people got lost in drugs. It all changed a lot.

Kronman: In a great sense, they won because they split us up, divided us. When I got out of jail, the last thing I wanted to do was to get back involved.

de la Rocha: But, in the end, we won. We stopped the war, brought Nixon to his knees, and changed a lot of how people live in the U.S.

FLACKS: I think that John Mitchell (Nixon's attorney general at the time) spent more time in jail than any of the protestors.

While this may have been the only bank to be burned to the ground, a lot of banks across the U.S. were being trashed.

BOB LANGFELDER
who spent six months in jail for activities during the bank burning

WHAT DID YOU LEARN FROM THOSE EXPERIENCES?

Langfelder: There were moments of great clarity in the '60s which we don't have in politics today. I'm sorry, but whether or not I.V. becomes a city or Gary Hart runs for Congress against Lagomarsino just doesn't compare with what we thought we had in our grasp. I'm a lot more middle class now -- into a monogamous relationship, own a home, and car, etc. But I probably would drop a lot of these commitments if, for example, the U.S. invaded Central America. I have become convinced that there are times in your life that you have to take risks to accomplish change, because in the cycle of life, things that you have to drop for a while will come back.

If I were to make one suggestion to today's students it would be to get off campus to take your politics into the community . . . Building and supporting "alternative" institutions . . . is even more relevant now than it was back then.

BECCA WILSON
former editor of the UCSB student newspaper

Kronman: I'm pretty happy with the direction my life has taken since then. It took me a while, but I'm now into writing, developing professional relationships -- although I'm surprised that I am a consultant to the County of Santa Barbara! [CL: In 2008, Kronman is Santa Barbara's Harbor Master]. I feel bad that many of us actually advocated on behalf of the North Vietnamese during the war, rather than just being antiwar, because I think this led to the bad treatment the Vietnam vets received when they got back.

Wilson: We didn't support the North Vietnamese government; we supported the National Liberation Front. And this, in my opinion, had nothing to do with why Vietnam vets were treated so shabbily. Frankly, I find myself today associating mostly with people who were activists in the '60s because there was a definite bonding among us that still exists today -- probably from the risks we took together even though we were in separate places in the country.

I don't live the radical life so much anymore; I don't insist on exposing the structural deficiencies of the capitalist system in my TV show, for example. But, I am nostalgic for the sense of community and the exhilaration we experienced back then.

If I were to make one suggestion to today's students it would be to get off campus -- to take your politics into the community. Building and supporting "alternative" institutions . . . is even more relevant now than it was back then.

Alex Berk, producer of the 1988 documentary interviewing Isla Vista activists from the 1970-era. Isla Vista *Free Press* photo.

The Causes of Conflict in Isla Vista

By David P. Gardner
Vice Chancellor, UCSB

Then Vice-Chancellor David P. Gardner wrote this statement for the "Chancellor's Special Report" dated April 3, 1970. Gardner was later president of the University of California (1975-89). I made the following excerpts of his statement. -- C.L.

Any assessment of the causes of conflict in Isla Vista must necessarily be more speculative than scientific. Comprehensive studies on the demography, economy, sociology, government, and physical environment of Isla Vista have simply not been done. . . .

This brief report, . . . nevertheless, (is) an attempt to state in a summary form what the administration understands to have been the primary causes of the Isla Vista disturbances of late February, 1970.

[T]here were multiple causes for the disorders. These were related to an array of national, state, local and University policies regarded by one or another group of students as mistaken at best, corrupt

-- and even criminal -- at worst. UCSB students are not importantly dissimilar from students enrolled elsewhere in California's universities and colleges in expressing discontent with the political mood of the State and in criticizing what they regard as the use of the University and state colleges by politicians and the news media for educationally irrelevant purposes. Thus, student confidence in the governmental and political processes has waned in recent years as has student respect for authority in general. At UCSB, many students have been for some time now psychologically and emotionally disposed toward more aggressive political behavior whenever the right combination of issues and circumstances occurred or could be arranged.

A number of specific local issues in January and February of this year were combined for the purpose of provoking a more overt expression of student resentment about the more general grievances already mentioned. The result was large-scale demonstrations in late January and early February on campus which culminated in the series of riotous evenings off campus in late February. These local issues were:

David P. Gardner, UCSB vice-chancellor in 1970. This picture was taken in 1988 when Gardner was president of the University of California. Isla Vista *Free Press* photo.

> *UCSB students are not importantly dissimilar from students enrolled elsewhere in California's universities and colleges in expressing discontent with the political mood of the State and in criticizing what they regard as the use of the University and state colleges by politicians and the news media for educationally irrelevant purposes.*
>
> DAVID P. GARDNER

* general dissatisfaction with the response of faculty and administration to student demands for a reconsideration and public hearing of the Allen case . . .

* a widespread and long-standing disquietude among many students in reference to the alleged slowness with which the University was moving to modify its structure so as to permit fuller student participation in educational decision-making of all kinds;

* a tightening of the academic job market for the first time in a quarter century raised the specter of "no vacancy" for junior members of the faculty not offered tenure and for graduate students seeking initial employment; and

* a potentially explosive situation in Isla Vista itself . . . especially in three critical areas:

   1) an extensive drug problem among youth everywhere, a particularly apparent problem in Isla Vista owing to the concentrated presence there of more than 10,000 young people, creates not only the

36

psychological and emotional problems associated with the widespread use of soft and hard drugs but also an aggravated relationship between many residents of Isla Vista and the law enforcement agencies involved;

2) an absence in Isla Vista of a variety of social outlets and an adult population prevents the natural development of normal social and community constraints on behavior thought essential to satisfactory community life. . . . it can be said that the typical Isla Vista resident (i.e., student) lives in an unencumbered social, ethical, and moral environment.

3) a critical dissimilarity of values between large numbers of students and some of the other Isla Vista residents and the values shared by the vast majority in the larger society, that is, differences about the value, worth, importance, and relevance of private property, personal responsibility, self-discipline, and permissiveness.

For example, . . . (t)he war in Vietnam outrages large numbers of students but not a comparable percentage of persons in the society in general, whereas the burning of the branch of the Bank of America outrages most persons in the larger community but not such large percentages of persons in Isla Vista.

> *. . . an absence in Isla Vista of a variety of social outlets and an adult population prevents the natural development of normal social and community constraints on behavior thought essential to satisfactory community life. . . . it can be said that the typical Isla Vista resident (i.e., student) lives in an unencumbered social, ethical, and moral environment.*
>
> DAVID P. GARDNER

These combinations of local issues, against a backdrop of general hostility toward state and national policies, provided ready tender for the militant or aggressive left to ignite in behalf of their own strategic objectives.

In this connection, the appearance of William Kunstler on the campus cannot be overlooked. Mr. Kunstler's presence attracted outside elements to the campus and to Isla Vista during a critical period and they, as well as his and the remarks of others from the platform, no doubt contributed to the scale and intensity of the disturbances.

The effect of campus radicals on the policies of the Legislative Council of the Associated Students and especially on those of the student newspaper throughout the fall and winter must also be taken into account. . . . [T]he radicals successfully interwove essentially separate issues into inseparable parts in the demonstrations on Dr. Allen's status so that effective, and credible faculty and administrative response on the more general question of student involvement in educational decision-making could not be separated from the Allen case.

. . . The Administration is all too frequently left with the potential of either acceding to ill-advised demands or of radicalizing a larger percentage of the student body by employing the use of outside police to effect security of the campus. The challenge has been to avoid being placed in the position of having to opt for either one or the other of these self-defeating possibilities.

There is now a clear trend to move such political activity into the community, . . . thus increasing the likelihood of both violence and property destruction.

. . . The trend is nationwide and should be carefully assessed by all of us.

There is now a clear trend to move such political activity into the community, . . . thus increasing the likelihood of both violence and property destruction. . . . The trend is nationwide and should be carefully assessed by all of us.

DAVID P. GARDNER

The Lessons of Isla Vista

By Louis B. Lundborg
Chairman of the Board, Bank of America

Lundborg was the author of three books: Future Without Shock *(1974),* Up to Now: The Story of an American Journey from Log Cabin to Board Room *(1978), and* The Art of Being an Executive *(1981). He also served on the Board of Directors of The Sierra Club (1971-74).*

The following excerpts are from a speech he delivered before the Seattle Rotary Club on June 17, 1970. Excerpted by Carmen Lodise.

On February 25, 1970, a rampaging mob of demonstrators — some students, some non-students — set fire to the Bank of America at Isla Vista, California, and totally destroyed it.

[H]ave we learned anything from our experience at Isla Vista? Can we see through and behind the burning of a bank there and behind all the continuing disturbances that keep flaring up there and elsewhere, to find any lesson in it, any consistent thread of principal to guide us?

. . . I think we can.

The . . . (lessons) are several, they are subtle, they are complex. (They) are easier to say in words than to follow in practice. But, . . . they are ignored at our peril. . .

1) Perhaps one of the greatest errors . . . has been the tendency to assume that all . . . the resultant disturbances, can be laid at the door of an extremely small fanatically militant hard-core minority of

students or even non-students. That such an assumption is comfortable in no way influences the fact that it is also grossly inaccurate.

While the actual burning of our Isla Vista branch may have been perpetrated by a violent few, there is no question that there was widespread agreement among the students of the Santa Barbara campus that the causes leading to the protest were both serious and legitimate.

2) There are many other issues than Vietnam. Having once been aroused by the war, having felt trapped into it by their elders, and impotent and frustrated in all their attempts to make themselves heard, these young people have begun to question everything their elders were doing; and to question everything about the society their elders created.

With so many involved, and feeling so deeply, the activist movement is not something fleeting that will go away if we can just keep it cool for awhile. And keep it cool we must, unless we want bloodshed . . . .

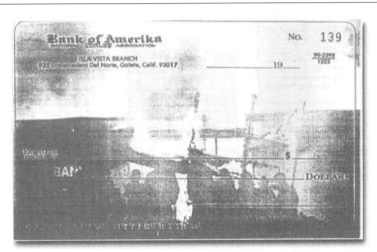

This is a photo of a bright orange and yellow, 2 ft. x 3 ft. poster showing the Isla Vista branch of the Bank of America in flames the night of February 25, 1970. The poster was created by Arthur Montez de Ocha, then head of the A.S. Print Shop, late that same night. It was on the street the next day, according to then-UCSB student Susan McClair, who assisted him in the project and whose personal check was used for the layout. It was popular at the time to spell America with a "k" in likening it to Nazi Germany. McClair went on to become a physician and practiced for several years at the Isla Vista Medical Clinic. This photo and story first appeared in IMAGES of the Isla Vista Medical Clinic, 1970-1995, which was written and edited by Carmen Lodise.

3) It won't be easy to cool it because we've already begun to choose up sides in ways that typically lead to trouble. We can see the polarizing taking shape with people on both sides tending to lump whole segments of the population together as "we" and "they" . . . .

4) The job of cooling it off is not made any easier by the fact that violence must be rejected and completely controlled, yet dissent and protest must not be rejected.

We can say, and I have said, that violence can be stopped by simple law and order methods. . . [B]ut those methods alone will not eliminate the seething that in the long run can cause us more difficulty than we have known up to now.

5) The young people may be upsetting us with their external appearances (long hair and

beards), but they are concerning themselves with more than the externals. And this is one of the basic reasons that the unrest won't soon go away. There is a new value system emerging in this country,

starting with the youth but not limited to them. It is becoming one of the new facts of life for the rest of us to deal with. It challenges basic assumptions that we not only have taken for granted, but that have virtually dominated our national life for most of our lives.

When Calvin Coolidge in 1925 said, "The business of America is business," a thoughtful people nodded "Why yes — that's right." Today's young people are saying, "That's not enough." Some are going further and saying; "Business is ruining America. Business is destroying our natural resources -- polluting our air and our water -- and why? To produce garbage -- things we don't need -- and must throw away to keep the economy going. It's a garbage economy, and we don't need it."

The people who are talking this way are not all hippies and are not all young . . . . [P]eople have come to regard the "system" as some kind of conspiracy. [but] Let's think about it:

The struggle for just the bare necessities dominated men's lives through most of history. Then, all of a sudden, just within one lifetime, have come all of the technological breakthroughs that change all that. It was not surprising that we should all get swept up in the excitement of producing — and in the excitement of the whole game of producing things.

This photograph, reproduced many times in many places without credit, is of graffiti painted on a Bank of America branch in Berkeley, Calif. on the 10th anniversary of the Isla Vista branch being burned to the ground.

. . . The ones who could do the most of that were the greatest heroes.

Now we wake up to realize that in the process of "conquering" nature, we were in fact destroying it -- and destroying part of our own lives with it.

For generations we have been mouthing the cliché, "You can't stand in the way of progress." Now there is a new generation that is saying, "The hell you can't." That generation and an increasing number of its elders -- are saying, "Prove to us that it really is progress." In a sense, that is the essence of everything that is stirring and boiling and seething: thoughtful people in increasing numbers are asking about one thing after another, "Is it really progress -- progress for the human condition?"

. . . And we shouldn't have to wait for them to ask the question -- because these should be our questions, too. This deterioration of the quality of life isn't something that just happens to other people; when it happens, it happens to us, too.

And because they think we are blind, or are refusing to see all these things that seem so plain to them, they are increasingly turning their backs on the things that we have said were important . . . . They don't know all of what they want -- that's part of why they are so confused and mixed up -- but they know they don't want that.

6) . . . (T)he final lesson -- what to do about it . . . . To this, I don't have all of the answers . . . only one or two.

The first one is to communicate; and it really calls for a second; open your minds and keep them open.

While the actual burning of our Isla Vista branch may have been perpetrated by a violent few, there is no question that there was widespread agreement among the students of the Santa Barbara campus that the causes leading to the protest were both serious and legitimate.

LOUIS B. LUNDBURG

I would suggest that . . . each of you find a college-age youth -- student or not -- and spend some time with him, to find out what's going on in that world that is crowding in on our heels.

There are many other issues than Vietnam. Having once been aroused by the war, having felt trapped into it by their elders, and impotent and frustrated in all their attempts to make themselves heard, these young people have begun to question everything their elders were doing; and to question everything about the society their elders created.

LOUIS B. LUNDBURG

And if you do, remember that God gave you two ears and only one tongue — use them in that proportion . . . . [A]s one who has tried it, let me say that it will be a sobering and maybe even a humbling experience . . . . [I]t will shock the pants off you, it will jar and shake most of the assumptions we all have grown up with.

. . . These (issues) aren't things that other people need, that other people want, that other people expect of us. These are for us -- we need the clean air, etc. -- for ourselves and our families.

They should be a part of our value system.

. . . [T]here are some hard-core radicals bent on the destruction of the "system" [and] . . . there is another group committed to the "system." But in between is the great, great majority of students and other young people, troubled, disturbed, questioning . . . waiting to be pulled either way. We can win them, if we are willing to work at it — if we are really willing to revolutionize the system from within -- in order to make it conform more closely with the value systems and needs of today -- rather than the value systems and needs of yesterday. In fact, we will be halfway home if they are convinced that we are really, sincerely willing to work at it.

We have two choices as to which way we can go . . . . One course will bring bloodshed, destruction and ultimate crushing of . . . the human spirit; the other course can bring peace and with it, a hope for the rekindling of the American Dream.

The hour is late; there isn't much time. But the choice is still ours.

LOUIS B. LUNDBURG

Because part of what lies at the root of their dissatisfaction, is the feeling that our generation just doesn't care about theirs.

We have two choices as to which way we can go. We can divide into camps and shoot it out; or we can try to find common grounds so that we can grow together again . . . . One course will bring bloodshed, destruction and ultimate crushing of . . . the human spirit; the other course can bring peace and with it, a hope for the rekindling of the American Dream.

The hour is late; there isn't much time. But the choice is still ours.

The struggle for just the bare necessities dominated men's lives through most of history. Then, all of a sudden, just within one lifetime, have come all of the technological breakthroughs that change all that. It was not surprising that we should all get swept up in the excitement of producing . . . . Now we wake up to realize that in the process of "conquering" nature, we were in fact destroying it. . .

LOUIS B. LUNDBURG

The Trow Report & UCSB's Responsibilities to Isla Vista

In April 1970, the UC Regents established a seven-person committee called The Commission on Isla Vista to "make recommendations for eliminating or ameliorating the causes of unrest in Isla Vista." The committee, which included UC Berkeley sociologist Martin Trow (after who the final report was popularly named) and Ira M. Heyman (former Professor of City & Regional Planning at UC Berkeley and Chancellor there from 1980 to 1990), chose "to make practical recommendations about the University's role in Isla Vista... [which were] designed to change the character

The Trow Report's observations and recommendations remain a standard by which the University's actions and policies toward Isla Vista can be judged.

of Isla Vista in ways that will reduce its potential for violence and destruction, and strengthen its potential as . . . a vital community."

The Commission made its final report to the UC Regents in October of that year.

The Trow Report's observations and recommendations remain a standard by which the University's actions and policies toward Isla Vista can be judged.

If there is one thread running through all of our deliberations and recommendations, it is that the University can no longer ignore, if it ever could, the conditions under which the bulk of its students live and spend the greater part of their time while at the University. What goes on in Isla Vista is as central to the University's life and functions as what goes on in its laboratories and lecture rooms.

THE TROW REPORT
Preface, p. iii

What follows are some selected excerpts from the Report's Preface and 100 pages of Observations and Recommendations, which are reproduced here in bold print.

I have also included COMMENTS as to what, to my knowledge, has been accomplished (and what has not) since the Trow Report was published. This analysis first appeared in the Isla Vista Free Press *on March 30, 1987 and has been partially updated for the publication of this book (2008).*

A fuller listing of Observations and Recommendations with Commentary can be found in Appendix A.

Note: On July 16, 2008 I wrote to UCSB Chancellor Henry T. Yang requesting assistance from him or his staff in updating the Trow Report for the publication of this book. On August 11, 2008, I received a polite email response from the chancellor wishing me well in this project and providing website links to sources that might help me to find the information I was seeking.

The chancellor's full response, including the links, are included in Appendix A. -- C.L.

SELECTED OBSERVATIONS

If there is one thread running through all of our deliberations and recommendations, it is that the University can no longer ignore, if it ever could, the conditions under which the bulk of its students live and spend the greater part of their time while at the University. What goes on in Isla Vista is as central to the University's life and functions as what goes on in its laboratories and lecture rooms. page iii, Preface.

The University cannot act in Isla Vista just as it does on its own campus; but neither can it refuse to act there at all. That principle, to which we have been persuaded by everything we have learned in our inquiry, is present in all of our recommendations. page iii, Preface.

. . . . (UCSB) has not enunciated and carried out an aggressive policy for dealing with the problems of Isla Vista. It has failed to intervene effectively in the pattern of Isla Vista land development, thereby allowing the conditions to arise in which dissatisfaction and frustration could flourish.

THE TROW REPORT
p. 85

Isla Vista is deeply scarred by the events of the past year . . . . Without indigenous institutions, the community can continue to be torn apart. But if increasing numbers of Isla Vista residents can feel that they are able to improve their own environment, Isla Vista can become a distinguished university community. Because of the unique local environment of Isla Vista, the ingredients are present for a promising experiment in community development. page 3

To the extent that UCSB has had a policy toward Isla Vista, it appears to have been to avoid extensive involvement in the affairs of the community. Until some official steps were taken recently to formulate a more aggressive policy, there was no statement of policy from the Chancellor specifying a philosophy of UCSB relationship to Isla Vista. page 55.

COMMENT: In anticipation of a statement like this in the forthcoming Trow Report, a UCSB policy toward Isla Vista was hurriedly written over the summer of 1970.

However, it was little adhered to and soon forgotten, as the statement in 1987 of Vice-Chancellor Edward Birch demonstrated (right).

COMMENT: Even several years later, it didn't appear that the Administration's attitude had changed much toward the community, as the comments of two subsequent chancellors, Daniel Aldrich and Barbara S. Uehling, indicate (see page 45).

"It's a mistake to think that there is one University policy toward the community, because there isn't the unanimity among the various parties here and we just don't have one, overall policy.

EDWARD BIRCH

Isla Vista *Free Press*
March 30, 1987

Edward Birch was UCSB Vice Chancellor of Student and Community Affairs during most of the years Robert Huttenback was chancellor. Birch was popularly known as "Fast Eddie" because he so often did differently than he pledged. Nevertheless, he went on to have a successful career in the private sector. Isla Vista *Free Press* photo by Keith Madigan.

Daniel Aldrich was the caretaker chancellor at UCSB between the firing of Robert Huttenback in 1986 and the hiring of Barbara Uehling in 1988. A decent man, he and his wife could often be seen strolling the beach and picking up trash. However, he just didn't get it when it came to Isla Vista. He's seen here being questioned by students about the University's commitment to diversity.

Isla Vista *Free Press* photograph.

"Isla Vista is not University campus; Isla Vista is contiguous to the campus. As such, the campus has to interact positively and sensitively with any community so close. The campus has to be a good neighbor, has to work constructively with the community."

DANIEL ALDRICH
Acting UCSB
Chancellor, 1986-87

I.V. *Free Press* interview.
March 30, 1987

"The University has a special responsibility to our students who live in I.V. But exercising this responsibility is difficult because ... we have no legal jurisdiction there."

BARBARA S.
UEHLING
UCSB Chancellor,
1988-94
I.V. *Free Press*
interview.
Feb. 15, 1989

New UCSB Chancellor Barbara Uehling being introduced at a press conference in 1988. The perky looking guy next to her is UC President David P. Gardner. Honest. Isla Vista *Free Press* photo.

Although she was the former chancellor of both the University of Missouri and Oklahoma State University, she soon got run off here by the UCSB faculty, who found her cold and uninvolved. Uehling never really tried to get to know Isla Vista and certainly gave no sign of having read the Trow Report.

A report to the Regents by the consulting firm of Pereira & Luckman in 1958 commented on Isla Vista's small lots narrow streets, lack of sidewalks and absence of street lights. Pereira & Luckman recommended that the University assist the county government in developing a "vital, well-balanced community, which will be most conducive to the University's healthy, long-term growth." It appears that no initiative was taken as a result of the recommendation. The County was not consulted for a joint land use plan for the area, and subsequent UCSB Long Range Plans in 1958, 1963, and 1968 basically ignored Isla Vista.

This was most striking in the 1963 and 1968 plans. By 1960 it was already apparent that students living off-campus would be seeking housing in Isla Vista, but this was not reflected in the 1963 plan. The University Planner in Berkeley reacted to this omission as follows:

"The seeming lack of concern for 'what goes on in Isla Vista' as evidenced by the Plan Study's lack of indication of land uses, circulation patterns, and current state of building development in this area, should be corrected at once. The campus obviously has a great stake in Isla Vista's growth coupled with and complementary to the campus itself for it is the campus' only residential neighbor. As at other campuses, intensive efforts must be made to coordinate physical planning of campus and community."

Again, alarming words went unheeded . . . . By 1968, the University almost completely surrounded Isla Vista, but the name "Isla Vista" appeared in passing only a few places in the 1968 UCSB Long-Range Development Plan. Perhaps symbolically, the maps included in that Report used nine colors to illustrate features of the campus and a stern gray to color Isla Vista, the airport and other "non-university" areas. pages 57-8.

The Commission believes (that there has been) . . . an inability on the part of the UCSB administration to

By 1960 it was already apparent that students living off-campus would be seeking housing in Isla Vista, but this was not reflected in the 1963 plan. The University Planner in Berkeley reacted to this omission as follows:

"The seeming lack of concern for 'what goes on in Isla Vista' . . . should be corrected at once. . . . As at other campuses, intensive efforts must be made to coordinate physical planning of campus and community."

Again, alarming words went unheeded . . . . By 1968, the University almost completely surrounded Isla Vista, but the name "Isla Vista" appeared in passing only a few places in the 1968 UCSB Long-Range Development Plan.

THE TROW REPORT
pp. 57-58

balance realistically and wisely its reluctance to intervene in affairs which affect the interests of private parties with the need to protect the orderly development of a University community in Isla Vista. page 66.

. . . the local [UCSB] administration's attitude that the improvement of Isla Vista's environment was of secondary importance in the long-range development of the campus . . . reflects a failure to consider the campus and Isla Vista as an integrated University community. page 67

In summary, in a situation that generates a great deal of misunderstanding and hostility, the University has made rather limited attempts to ameliorate tensions or improve living conditions. At the same time, the University continues to expand its enrollment without providing additional attractive living quarters on campus. In a sense, UCSB is the most powerful 'citizen' in Isla Vista, yet in our opinion it has refused to assume its proportionate civic responsibility. page 76.

SELECTIVE RECOMMENDATIONS (pp. 85-100)

#1A. That UCSB adopt and take immediate steps to implement policies recognizing that Isla Vista is an integral part of the University community and that UCSB's vital interests are involved in improving the quality of life there.

> Rationale: UCSB has a vital interest in Isla Vista; its campuses virtually surround the area; approximately two-thirds of its student body lives in Isla Vista; . . . the functioning of UCSB as an educational institution is greatly affected by events occurring in Isla Vista.

> *. . . the local [UCSB] administration's attitude that the improvement of Isla Vista's environment was of secondary importance in the long-range development of the campus . . . reflects a failure to consider the campus and Isla Vista as an integrated University community. . . .*
>
> *. . . . In a sense, UCSB is the most powerful 'citizen' in Isla Vista, yet in our opinion it has refused to assume its proportionate civic*
>
> THE TROW REPORT

The Commission believes that the unique relationship of UCSB and Isla Vista requires a higher degree of University involvement in local affairs . . . . (UCSB) has not enunciated and carried out an aggressive policy for dealing with the problems of Isla Vista. It has failed to intervene effectively in the pattern of Isla Vista land development, thereby allowing the conditions to arise in which dissatisfaction and frustration could flourish.

Recent events indicate the need for leadership to aid in the creation of a sub-structure of community institutions upon which a more stable community can be built.

Specifically: that the Chancellor of UCSB take immediate steps to create an administrative office, properly staffed, to implement a policy of UCSB involvement . . . . utilizing the funds allocated by The Board of Regents on September 19, 1970, for the purpose of providing a community affairs officer and other services.

Additional funding should be provided by the Regents as necessary.

COMMENT: The Regents initially allocated several hundred thousand dollars. Most of these so-called Regents Funds went to policing and administration, but an important chunk went to nurture the development of several community institutions, including the Isla Vista Community Council (IVCC), Open Door Medical Clinic, Community Federal Credit Union, Youth Project/Children's Center, etc. See the chart on page 49.

However, Chancellor Robert Huttenback's administration (1979-86) took the view that this was intended as "seed money" rather than as funds to be provided "as necessary" as the Trow Report explicitly recommended, and all of this funding was discontinued in 1983 -- without advance warning to these community agencies and without any UC Regent-level discussion.

Even before 1983 the UCSB Administration was backing off its commitment to the community. Note that for the period 1976-1982 the allocation to the UCSB Administration to administer UC Regents funding of Isla Vista community programs exceeded the total distributed to community-run agencies (CC plus C) and that for the three-year period 1983-85 the UCSB Administration allocated over $85,500 to itself for administering no programs.

> *Without indigenous institutions, the community can continue to be torn apart. But if increasing numbers of Isla Vista residents can feel that they are able to improve their own environment, Isla Vista can become a distinguished university community. Because of the unique local environment of Isla Vista, the ingredients are present for a promising experiment in community development.*
>
> THE TROW REPORT

RECOMMENDATION: This vice-chancellor must have authority to initiate and coordinate UCSB services that relate directly to Isla Vista.

Specifically: that UCSB work with community organizations to upgrade the physical condition of Isla Vista, and that UCSB help in the building of community institutions, including: services to students available where they live (i.e., in Isla Vista), . . . [and] continue UCSB's active role in the development of the Isla Vista Community Center . . . (and) develop similar student-oriented services as new or different community needs become clear.

UC Funding of all Isla Vista Programs, 1969-85

(in dollars)

Year	CC	C	FP	Adm	AO	Total
1969	0	0	0	0	0	0
1970	0	6,232	19,310	48,232	0	73,774
1971	13,769	136,064	58,673	59,702	0	268,983
1972	28,294	151,498	72,515	39,223	0	330,753
1973	33,562	51,425	85,800	34,949	*105,500	313,236
1974	29,086	44,151	118,071	41,200	15,800	248,308
1975	24,177	38,804	143,703	34,392	0	241,076
1976	25,035	21,821	184,491	47,611	0	278,958
1977	9,283	5,762	165,478	51,595	0	232,118
1978	6,951	36,873	158,209	70,553	0	272,586
1979	9,312	28,606	212,296	78,815	0	329,029
1980	9,037	6,138	247,034	21,084	0	238,338
1981	9,000	928	236,040	30,345	0	276,313
1982	9,000	0	254,768	32,266	0	296,034
1983	0	0	0	37,347	0	37,347
1984	0	0	0	47,496	0	47,496
1985	0	0	0	670	0	670

* includes $69,500 contributed personally by UC Regent Norton Simon

C = Isla Vista Community Council
CC = all other Isla Vista community agencies
FP = Foot Patrol policing
Adm = UCSB Administration of these programs
AO = Anisq'Oyo Park acquisition, development

SOURCE: UCSB Office of Planning & Research, 1987

COMMENT: Initially, Regents Funds and a small grant from the Bank of America funded several programs that were able to rent out most of the space of the two buildings at 966 & 970 Embarcadero Del Mar in Isla Vista. Today, 966 contains several restaurants including the Cantina, Deja Vu, Rosarito, and Naan Stop, while 970 was purchased by the Isla Vista Open Door Medical Clinic in 1977 with a grant of federal funds allocated by the County of Santa Barbara and secured by the Isla Vista Community Council.

During the late-1970s, while IVCC was attempting to secure funding to purchase both buildings for the bargain price of $140,000, the UCSB Administration twice refused to contribute $50,000 to the project — once from a student registration fee surplus that at the time was over $4 million. The recommendation from a student committee to allocate $50,000 of this surplus to purchase the Isla Vista Service Center buildings was vetoed by then-Chancellor Robert Huttenback.

COMMENT: Note that for the period 1976-1982 the allocation to the UCSB Administration to administer UC Regents funding of Isla Vista community programs exceeded the total distributed to community-run agencies (CC & C) and that for the three-year period 1983-85 the UCSB Administration allocated over $85,000 to itself for administering no programs.

The community was lucky to wind up with one of the buildings, which was purchased with federal Housing and Community Development funds through the County when Jim Slater was supervisor (1972-76), but for a price of $105,000. See Chapter 11.

RECOMMENDATION #2. That UCSB both initiate and seek the cooperation of others in initiating programs to create a more varied community in Isla Vista.

Rationale: UCSB should take the lead in working with residents of Isla Vista to develop a community marked by a greater diversity of age, occupations, interests, and other personal characteristics.

Specifically: the University should actively investigate the feasibility of establishing one or more small residential colleges in existing housing in Isla Vista, and it should locate in Isla Vista more UCSB cultural and academic activities.

COMMENT: The first recommendation was never followed, and the second exists to the extent that UCSB began some of these suggested activities in 1988 after they purchased the Magic Lantern Theater in Isla Vista. The Magic Lantern's name was changed to the Isla Vista Theater. It is used primarily as a lecture hall, but it does have movies and some live entertainment several evenings per week. In 2002, the University leased and remodeled the rebuilt Bank of America building and converted it into a lecture hall with some space for studying and meetings.

Specifically: the University should construct apartments (attractive to students with children) in Isla Vista or on parts of its campus adjacent to that part of Isla Vista in which most UCSB students live, (and) encourage faculty members and University employees to live in Isla Vista and to become involved with students and others in community.

COMMENT: Since 1970, UCSB has constructed the Santa Ynez housing project and new married students housing, not on the main campus as recommended by the Trow Report but on Storke Campus.

The IVCC urged the administration to site its new faculty housing project on Main Campus, on the bluff adjacent to Del Playa Dr. The I.V. Park District even offered to trade some land in Isla Vista for the project for exactly the reasons suggested in the Trow Report. Instead, the project was sited on a large section of open space on UCSB's West Campus.

> *The recommendation from a student committee to allocate $50,000 of this surplus to purchase the Isla Vista Service Center buildings was vetoed by then-Chancellor Robert Huttenback.*

RECOMMENDATION #3. That UCSB, the County, and members of the community cooperate to develop programs to provide increased and improved services in Isla Vista.

Rationale: Many forms of municipal services are deficient or completely lacking in Isla Vista.
Specifically: the University should give immediate attention to establishing greater UCSB-County cooperation — in the context of Isla Vista community involvement — to provide appropriate services for Isla Vista .... [especially] to develop and staff park and recreational facilities in that area of Isla Vista most heavily populated by students.

COMMENT: In 1974, UC Regents' Funds began being supplemented by county revenue sharing funds for social services and general funds for the IVCC. I am not personally aware of any major UCSB involvement in this process; primarily it was these fledgling organizations finding new resources on their own.

However, there was major assistance from the university in the purchase and development of Aniso'Oyo Park in the center of Isla Vista. Although the bulk of the funds for the $480,000 project came from the federal government, the UC Regents contributed about $50,000; then UC Regent Norton Simon personally contributed an additional $69,500.

And UCSB loaned its campus planner to the IVCC's planning department for two years (1972-74). During his tenure, John Robert Henderson taught dozens of residents basic land-use planning and how these might apply in Isla Vista. He also assisted in the development of a community plan, which was published in 1973 as <u>Recommendations for Isla Vista Planning</u>, and designed Anisq'Oyo Park.

After almost no involvement in Isla Vista from 1983 through 1988, a new initiative began in 1989 with the opening of a campus/country/community office in the Isla Vista Open Door Medial Clinic's building, which was being expanded to 3,000 square feet. UCSB hired a full-time liaison that was in charge of new programs there. However, this office was moved to Embarcadero Hall when it opened in 2004.

RECOMMENDATIONS #4 & 5. Increase the effectiveness of policing in Isla Vista *(paraphrased: C.L.).*

Rationale: . . . . Repetition of the violence of the past would seriously undermine the potential effectiveness of all of our recommendations, which ultimately seek to build a sense of community. Should violence recur in the future, however, it must be met effectively and in ways that minimize the creation of hostility among the vast majority of Isla Vista residents who do not engage in violent acts. We believe that innovative approaches and procedures to police problems in Isla Vista are needed.

Specifically: that UCSB, local police forces, and community representatives immediately create a police liaison committee for Isla Vista to be charged with developing plans for dealing with major disorders, . . . that the University encourage community involvement in actual policing activities (and) . . . that the proposed police foot patrol in Isla Vista be implemented . . . as soon as possible.

COMMENT: It is with policing activities that one could say the university and the County have best cooperated to fulfill the recommendations of the Trow Report. The County sheriff secured a federal grant to commence a foot and bike patrol operation in late 1970. The university paid for half of this innovative policing operation from UC Regent funds. The Foot Patrol continues through today. See Chapter 13.

However, funding for UCSB's share was shifted from administration monies to student fees under Chancellor Robert Huttenback (1977-86). Acting-Chancellor Aldrich phased it back to administration sources over three years beginning in 1987.

Trow Report recommendations not followed include the active recruitment of Isla Vista community members for sworn personnel, and some kind of empowered police/community committee to review police activities. However, the IVCC had a very active police commission for most of the 1970s, although it seldom had any cooperation from the police.

RECOMMENDATION #6. That the University provide recreational and housing facilities for Isla Vista residents.

Specifically: that UCSB should . . . formulate a standard lease though the cooperative efforts of UCSB, students, and Isla Vista property owners and managers, with a view toward reaching an agreement adopted by all major landlords in Isla Vista.

COMMENT: Although some work was done on this project, such a lease did not exist as of this writing (2008) according to the UCSB Community Housing Office.

Specifically: that the University develop contingency plans for additional apartment-style housing on campus . . . (and) encourage and assist interested community groups in the formation of student housing cooperatives . . . .

COMMENT: There was minimal activity on these recommendations for years. Only the new family student housing and the Santa Ynez complex on Storke Campus were added in the 1970s. Then nothing much happened in the 1980s and '90s.

The University did help maintain and expand the Rochdale Housing Co-op after it was started by students. However, soon after it became involved, the Administration converted it to a student-only program — hardly in line with this recommendation.

To be fair, the University has significantly expanded university-owned housing beginning in the late 1990s. First, the University bought two large apartment complexes in Isla Vista and converted them to student housing in the late 1980s, which hold about 575 residents. In about 2005, they bought Francisco Torres Residence Hall on El Colegio Road at Storke Road, which holds 1,325 UCSB students, and changed its name to Santa Catalina Residence Hall.

However, all of this additional housing is restricted to student occupancy, which certainly violates the intent of the Trow Commission recommendation. In addition, this has taken housing for nearly 2,000 people out of the private sector available to non-students, so it hasn't really taken pressure off the limited supply of housing in Isla Vista.

Other additional student housing projects include the Manzanita Village (800 students) on the bluff top on Main Campus near Isla Vista and the just-opened San Clemente Residence Hall (964 students) in what were once open playing fields along El Colegio Road.

Still, because UCSB student enrollment has increased by 8,884, or 71%, since 1973 (from 12,526 to 21,410 in the fall of 2007 according to the UCSB Office of Budget and Planning), there is a real question as to whether these efforts have been sufficient. These additional dwelling units have absorbed only 40% of the added students and only 10% (3,652 of 35,536) of the total population impact of this additional enrollment, when the multiplier effect is factored in. Note: UCSB's 1974 Long Range Development Plan estimated that an additional three-to-four persons are added to the local population for each additional student (8,884 x 4 = 35,536).

For an in-depth look at how UCSB enrollment practices have impacted Isla Vista, see pages 62-65 and Chapter 14.

Specifically: that the University use portions of the main campus adjacent to Isla Vista for parks and playing fields (because) . . . efforts must be made to blend the dead-end streets of Isla Vista into the campus so that the feeling of a barrier now present there is

eliminated . . . (and) priority should be given to construction of the projected University Student Center . . . adjacent to Isla Vista.

COMMENT: Neither of these recommendations was followed. However, there are several projects being contemplated in the upcoming Long Range Development Plan (2010) that would ease the transition between Main Campus and the town.

RECOMMENDATION #7. That in view of the present level of services available to UCSB and Isla Vista, we believe the optimum size of student population has been exceeded. And until such time as our recommendations can be implemented and their effected evaluated, the present size of the student body should be maintained.

COMMENT: The Trow Report has never been evaluated by the University of California as to which, if any, of the report's recommendations were adopted, and what, if any effect the recommendations might have had.

In 1983 IVCC asked the UC Regents to establish a committee to undertake such a review. This request was denounced before the Regents by then-Chancellor Robert Huttenback as a "red herring." UC President David Gardner (by coincidence, a vice-chancellor at UCSB in 1970) did not support such a review. Despite a heated discussion for several minutes, the Regents never voted on the request; basically, they just ignored it.

Of course, UCSB has not maintained its enrollment; it has increased it by 56% -- from 13,733 in 1969 to 21,410 in 2007 -- and the Long Range Development Plan currently under review (2008) calls for an enrollment of 25,000 by 2025 -- although UCSB analysts readily admit they don't yet know where they will find enough water to support this added population.

RECOMMENDATION #8. That the University-wide Administration take action to provide resources to UCSB to implement the recommendations of this report.

<u>Rationale:</u> Both the University-wide administration and UCSB have failed to muster and use the resources available to them to anticipate and to meet the problems in Isla Vista. We believe that the planning of UCSB as a campus and in its relation to Isla Vista has been inadequate and that immediate action must be given to taking actions that will guard against the repetition of past mistakes.

COMMENT: These funds were made available for the years 1970-83, then abruptly terminated. See the chart on page 49.

FINAL COMMENT: Overall, it's fair to ask whether UCSB has continued to take "actions that will guard against the repetition of past mistakes".

CHAPTER 4

BUILDING A COMMUNITY

One of the major conclusions of all of the studies of what happened in Isla Vista in the years 1969 and '70 was that Isla Vista residents felt powerless to affect public policies both nationally and locally. They were perpetual victims of political and economic forces beyond their control. And the complicity of the UCSB administration and the County in creating these circumstances was too painfully obvious.

Thus, it wasn't the riots that created a community out of Isla Vista; it was what happened in response to the riots, as residents joined together to create and sustain organizations that insulated them from the harshest of outside political and economic forces. Across the nation, young people were developing an "alternative life-style" to a Corporate Amerika whose pollution was killing the planet and whose international quest for resources continually immersed it in imperialistic wars. "Youth Culture" is what UCSB Sociology Professor Dick Flacks termed this rapidly emerging alternative society in his widely read book by the same title.

Activists of the time felt that here was a little piece of the planet in which -- with a lot of hard work -- they could build a viable and semi-independent community whose institutions would reflect the new values of the youth culture.

In Isla Vista, with its heavy concentration of young people, and with the solidarity among them forged in the intensity of the six months of civil strife, this idealism unleashed a community-building and self-determination movement that would characterize the town for many years.

Activists of the time felt that here was a little piece of the planet in which -- with a lot of hard work -- they could build a viable and semi-independent community whose institutions would reflect the new values of the youth culture.

The vision was one of a community as a laboratory of social change: a training ground for its continually revolving citizens -- young, idealistic, with few vested interests -- who were coming in contact with the newest ideas in Western civilization at one of its better universities, and also getting a hands-on education building new institutions.

These residents (upon graduation) would be shot like missiles out into the larger society as experienced change agents -- harbingers of a new society in the making. This was a most radical, yet very peaceful plan for creating a new America.

Like a phoenix rising out of the fire that consumed the Bank of America building -- the most obvious symbol in town of the dominant culture -- Isla Vista's unique experiment began to be implemented.

IVCC Formed

Isla Vista was certainly a challenge for these erstwhile world-changers.

The vision was one of a community as a laboratory of social change: a training ground for its continually revolving citizens -- young, idealistic, with few vested interests -- who were coming in contact with the newest ideas in Western civilization at one of its better universities, and also getting a hands-on education building new institutions.

These residents (upon graduation) would be shot like missiles out into the larger society as experienced change agents -- harbingers of a new society in the making. This was a most radical, and yet very peaceful plan for creating a new America.

Isla Vista Profiles
(U.S. Census data, except where noted)

	1980	1990*	2000*
Population	14,500	20,395	18,344
	(excludes UCSB)	(includes UCSB)	(includes UCSB)
Dwelling Units	4,440	5,151	5,264
% renters	96.0%	96.0%	95.6%
Median rents	$300/bed**	n.a.	$842
ages: 18-29	79.1%		
ages: 15-24		77.5%	75.0%
Low-income HH	76.0%		
HH <$25,000		72.4%	65.1%
Bikes/Capita	1.04***	n.a.	n.a.

* Beginning in 1990, the Isla Vista CDP included the UCSB campus and housing units between Storke & Los Carneros roads north to Hollister Ave.

** highest in Santa Barbara County

*** Isla Vista Community Council research

Note: The County Planning Department estimated that as many as 5% of Isla Vista residents were missed in the 2000 Census. For example, only one homeless person was counted. Also, while the number of dwelling units increased from 1990, the total population estimate declined.

More than 11,000 people, over two-thirds of who were students at UCSB, lived in barely one-half square mile, not including the 1,325 who live at Francisco Torres (now Santa Catalina) Residence Hall, which went vacant in the early 1970s as UCSB enrollment dropped by one-tenth by 1972. More than 96% of these residents were renters, 33% of the town was paved-over, there were no social services, and neither the County nor UCSB had any presence in I.V. Where to begin was even a challenge.

First, residents came together politically with the formation of the Isla Vista Community Council (IVCC). At a time when County officials were actively resisting attempts by students to register to vote at their campus address, more than 4,000 residents voted in

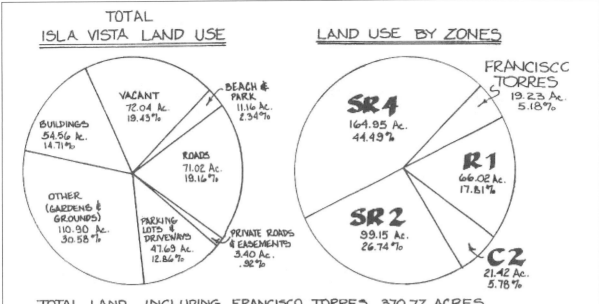

TOTAL
ISLA VISTA LAND USE

LAND USE BY ZONES

VACANT
72.04 Ac.
19.43%

BEACH &
PARK
11.16 Ac.
2.34%

BUILDINGS
54.56 Ac.
14.71%

ROADS
71.02 Ac.
19.16%

OTHER
(GARDENS &
GROUNDS)
110.90 Ac.
30.58%

PARKING
LOTS &
DRIVEWAYS
47.69 Ac.
12.86%

PRIVATE ROADS
& EASEMENTS
3.40 Ac.
.92%

FRANCISCO
TORRES
19.23 Ac.
5.18%

SR4
164.95 Ac.
44.49%

R1
66.02 Ac.
17.81%

SR2
99.15 Ac.
26.74%

C2
21.42 Ac.
5.78%

TOTAL LAND, INCLUDING FRANCISCO TORRES, 370.77 ACRES

Isla Vista Land Use, 1972. At the end of the development ogre that characterized Isla Vista in the 1960s, Isla Visa was roughly 33% paved over with only 72 acres remaining undeveloped. Through the 1970s, '80s, and '90s, the community was able to purchase roughly 57 of those acres primarily through the Isla Vista Recreation & Park District, with some major assistance from the Isla Vista Redevelopment Agency, a County agency. Source: Recommendations for Isla Vista Planning, 1973.

the first IVCC elections held May 5, 1970. Only 3,400 residents were officially registered to vote at the time, when the law still required people to be 21 to vote.

However, IVCC rules allowed any resident age 16 or over to vote for council members. IVCC elections were carried out by 70-80 volunteers, who were permitted to set up tables outside of County polling places during official elections. IVCC ballots were handed out to voters as they entered the County polling place, then returned to the IVCC tables out front. Ballots were hand-counted that evening, usually over beer and pizza donated by local merchants.

The Council saw its mission to be the establishment of a consensus on important issues facing the community through public hearings and referendums, then to lobby for adoption of such policies by the empowered governmental-bodies, that is, the UCSB administration and County government.

Secondly, while both the County and UCSB officials were vitriolic in their condemnation of the actions of individual demonstrators, the

The First Isla Vista Community Council
Elected May 5, 1970

Greg Knell
Jon Wheatley
Dan Kennedy
Walter Chesnavich
Bruce Macvicar
Joe Cardinale
Robert Conner
Richard Duprey
Chris Loizeaux
Debi Graff
Geoffrey Wallace

several studies done on the causes of the riots so unanimously criticized the roles played by both of these governmental agencies, that each began to respond quite positively to suggestions on how to ameliorate living conditions in Isla Vista. The County even placed a moratorium on more building in Isla Vista — although this wasn't much of a concession because UCSB enrollment dropped in the fall of 1970 as some parents kept their children away from this politically unstable area.

UC Regents Funding

Much to everyone's surprise, the UC Regents allocated over $750,000 in a three-year plan to assist in getting several community organizations off the ground. "Tribute money," some people called it — an insurance premium paid to end the rioting. Nonetheless, it was through such Regents Opportunity Funds that the Isla Vista Open Door Medical Clinic, the Isla Vista Credit Union, and the Isla Vista Community Council (IVCC) obtained important start-up money, which continued for several years. See page 49. Also, the UC Regents and the County jointly funded an experimental "foot patrol" policing function in Isla Vista, although the County's share came from a federal grant. Even the Bank of America threw in $15,000 toward the renting of an Isla Vista Service Center building at 970 Embarcadero del Mar, which housed many of Isla Vista's first community programs. See Chapter 11.

In 1972, the County recognized the elected IVCC as the official representatives of the community (the Isla Vista Municipal Advisory Council) and proclaimed Isla Vista the official name of the town, recognizing it as a separate community from Goleta.

Following over 100 hours of public hearings, the body of work developed under the guidance of Henderson was approved by the 1972-73 IVCC and published in 1973 in a 120-page document with nearly 50 illustrations as Recommendations for Isla Vista Planning.

Citizen Participation

Probably the most important aspect of the money provided by the UC Regents -- even more than the amount -- was the fact that most of it came without strings attached. A community group was formed to advise the University how this money should be spent, and the advice was followed for the most part. The IVCC was given an annual grant of $25,000 to spend as its elected representatives saw fit.

In addition, the University paid the salary of a full-time architect, John Robert Henderson, the UCSB Campus Planner for the previous eight years, who moved into the IVCC offices and assisted the community to democratically develop a long-range plan for physical improvements and the eventual down-zoning of the town from a build-out capacity of 44,000 people to 24,000. This approach increased the sense of empowerment of Isla Vista residents and a broad base of the population felt a sense of involvement and ownership in the creation and maintenance of these new agencies and in the community planning process.

Following over 100 hours of public hearings, the body of work developed under the guidance of Henderson was approved by the 1972-73 IVCC and published in 1973 in a 120-page document with

ISLA VISTA PLANNING VISIONS

GOALS	HOW	NOW
Local government	Local, legal control over critical government processes, including police, planning, building and housing, and animal control.	Park and Recreation District, Municipal Advisory Council, choice by community of College Community Services District or cityhood.
To provide the privilege of being a non-polluting citizen in a non-polluting community.	Preserve open space, drastically reduce motor vehicles, promote recycling and greening, minimize resource depletion and energy transformation.	Implementation of Transportation Plan accepted by IVCC to minimize car traffic and encourage bike and pedestrian traffic; Ecology Action Recycling Center.
To provide a safe, beautiful and esthetic environment.	Noise reduction, car reduction, promote public transportation, tree planting, parks, murals, benches and prevent population growth.	Madrid Park, Window to the Sea, barrier parks, curb bulbs, street trees, murals, and working on bikeways, trams and zone changes.
To be a highly developed cultural and educational community.	Promote recreation, entertainment, instruction in the esoteric and the arts, and promote community participation and interest in local government.	Recreational Activities Office in IVCSC, People's Arts Program, Development of I.V. oriented classes at the University, IVCC Newsletter, pamphlets, posters.
To engender economic balance and maximize community self-sufficiency.	Local ownership and management of business and housing; crafts, services, and housing co-ops; non-polluting industry, home gardens, agriculture.	Isla Vista Community Service Center, I.V. Crafts Fairs, organic gardens, working on Community Development Corporations.
To fully interact as a mature community with all other communities.	Increased communication with other neighborhoods and communities, and increased interaction with local governments.	Participation in Goleta Valley Government Group, Goleta Valley Citizens Planning Group, County Water District.
To promote a heterogeneous population with amenities for all.	More single family housing, natural beauty, better public services and family oriented community activities, stable year-round population.	Approval of some buildings in R-1 area, I.V. Youth Project, I.V. Kids Korps, Well-Baby Clinic.

Developed and adopted by the 1972-73 Isla Vista Community Council nearly 50 illustrations as <u>Recommendations for Isla Vista Planning</u>. These recommendations are summarized in **Isla Vista Planning Visions**, reprinted here on page 59.

At the time, the IVCC offices were at 966C Embarcadero del Mar (where The Cantina restaurant is now). For several years, the IVCC office was the hub of community development activities. IVCC meetings ran past midnight each Monday, and Planning, Police, and Animal Control commissions met weekly. Literally hundreds of students took independent study courses, examining new schemes to rid the town of cars, create parks, new organizations, and new forms of governance. More than fifteen original studies of the community's physical layout, demographic profile, and proposed new programs were published during the early 1970s — most funded with UC Regents funds allocated by the IVCC.

Other Community Organizations

The new Council began to create other options. For example, IVCC's Planning Commission developed and implemented the beginnings of a bikeway system and other auto-reduction programs. The Planning Commission also negotiated the student bus pass system with the Santa Barbara Metropolitan Transit Authority in which UCSB students pay a low fixed-cost per quarter through student fees and ride the bus free; the system still operates today. The Planning Commission also designed and oversaw the construction of Anisq'Oyo Park, which was funded primarily by the federal government but granted to the Isla Vista Recreation and Park District.

1972-73 Isla Vista Community Council. Bottom row, left to right: Trish Davey, Steve Logan, JoAnne Yokota. Middle: Leslie McFadden, Bill Wallace. Top: Carmen Lodise, Al Plyley, Bob Martin. Absent: Dr. Dave Bearman.

The Isla Vista Park District itself was also initiated by IVCC's Planning Commission. Established by a citizen-vote in late 1972, the Park District remains today the only official local government unit with taxing authority completely controlled by I.V. residents; its five-member board of directors is elected by the registered voters of Isla Vista (excluding residents of the UCSB campus and Francisco Torres [Santa Catalina] Residents Hall) to staggered four-year terms in Novembers of even-numbered years. When the district was formed, there was only one park in Isla Vista -- Ocean View Park on Del Playa Drive at Camino Corto Road. See Chapter 6.

These organizations eventually took on a life of their own:

* Isla Vista voters in 1975 passed a $1,150,000 park bond measure (coincidentally, or perhaps ironically, the same amount of money that Tom Storke was paid when he sold his land to the UC Regents for what is now Storke Campus) and the Isla Vista Park District, that is, the community, is now

the biggest landowner in town.

Other organizations sprang up in that period, most resulting from a special committee of the IVCC:

* The IVCC in 1976 obtained a grant that allowed the Medical Clinic to purchase the Isla Vista Service Center building at 970 Embarcadero del Mar, a building that underwent an expansion in the late 1980s that doubled its size. See Chapter 11.

> *Probably the most important aspect of the money provided by the UC Regents -- even more than the amount -- was the fact that most of it came without strings attached.*

* The Youth Project and Children's Center are now one organization, but it moved to Goleta in 2005.

* The Human Relations Center moved to Goleta but eventually transformed itself into the Carpinteria-based Pacific Institute.

* The Isla Vista Food Co-op is still going strong, but the Credit Union discontinued operating in the early 2000s.

CETA and CDBG Funding

In the mid-1970s, federal job-training (CETA) and community development (CDBG) funding became available through the County. At one point, more than 50 people had CETA positions working in Isla Vista's new agencies, getting important, hands-on employment experience in these democratically run organizations while helping to build the community.

Even the County got involved when they hired two I.V. residents as CETA workers to be I.V.'s dogcatchers in an attempt to curtail the packs of dogs that had become a danger to children. These animal control trainees were permitted to use special enforcement rules developed by the IVCC's Animal Control Commission. Dogs had to be within voice control of their owners, not leashed as required elsewhere in the county. Three citations for wandering

---

Isla Vista's Earliest Community Institutions

Isla Vista Association
(IVA) 1968

Isla Vista Community Council
(IVCC) 1970

Isla Vista Open Door Medical Clinic 1970

Isla Vista Community Federal Credit Union 1971

IVCC Planning Commission
1971

Isla Vista Government Study
1971

Isla Vista Recreation & Park District (IVRPD) 1972

IVCC Police Commission
1973

IVCC Animal Control Commission 1973

Isla Vista Youth Project
1973

Isla Vista Children's Center 1973

Isla Vista Food Co-op
1974

Isla Vista Human Relations Center (IVHRC) 1974

Isla Vista Housing Co-op
(later the Rochdale Housing Co-op)
1975

---

without such voice control meant the dog had to be removed from town.

In less than a year, the two CETA-dogcatchers had the situation under control -- proving that, at least in some areas, Isla Vistans could do a better job running the town than the County.

It was both the initiation of these community institutions and the support they received from local residents that created the basis of the "community" of Isla Vista. In just a few years, a whole collection of new institutions were established that attempted to relate to residents' basic needs and to represent their opinions and aspirations to outside authorities.

Isla Vista CETA dog catchers K.C. Swarztel (left) and David Hoskinson. In 1975-76, the County allowed Isla Vista to establish its own rules for animal control enforcement and the problem of roving dog packs was solved within a year. UCSB *Daily Nexus* photograph used with permission.

Isla Vistans were no longer powerless and for awhile there seemed no limit to the possibilities of what lay ahead.

UCSB Over-Enrollment

The scramble for living space in I.V. became intense between 1972 and 1982 when UCSB began ratcheting up its enrollment, while the total number of dwelling units remained approximately the same -- due to a moratorium on new construction enacted by Isla Vista and Goleta voters in 1972 because the area had run out of water. See Chapter 10.

UCSB fall enrollment – the figure that establishes rental contracts for the full school year – which was just under 3,000 in 1959, had increased roughly 1,000/year to 13,733 in 1969. See the chart on page 64: UCSB Enrollment Levels, 1954-2006. However, UCSB enrollment fell back considerably after the 1970 civil disturbances to 12,300 by 1972. Therefore, the number of people (especially students) living in Isla Vista declined, which drove down rents considerably. During this period, many families and non-students moved into Isla Vista and the percentage of college students dropped from over 75% of the town to roughly 44%, much as the 1970 Trow Report had recommended.

But total enrollment increased by 751 in 1973 and another 1,307 students in 1974. Astoundingly, a special census conducted by the County in early 1975 found only five vacant apartments in Isla Vista out of a total of more than 4,400 household units, as vacancy signs became an endangered species. Rents increased in double-digit percentage points each year from 1974 through 1980.

And, of course, I.V.'s absentee landlords cashed in on the situation big-time. A study done by the UCSB *Daily Nexus* in 1978, the year following the implementation of Proposition 13, which limited property tax rates, found that total property taxes paid went down $2 million in Isla Vista that year, while total rents paid went up $2 million — netting the absentee

. . . vacancy signs became an endangered species [and] rents increased in double-digit percentage points each year from 1974 through 1980.

Richard Jensen, whose enrollment projections for UCSB were always wrong. I.V. *Free Press* photo.

landlords a nifty $4 million.

It didn't get any better in the 1980s. By 1989, UCSB's enrollment level exceeded 19,000, which was far in excess of the 13,750 limit recommended in the Trow Report and 3,609 over the level in 1978. Richard Jensen, the UCSB official in charge of projecting enrollment for the upcoming fall during that period, missed so badly on the low side each year that his estimates became a joke.

However, the only additional new housing construction in I.V. between 1972 and 1989 was the Santa Ynez Apartments on Storke Campus, which holds about 600 people, and the fifty houses in Isla Vista built during 1989 with Measure T water permits, which held perhaps another 500 people. And because three-to-four additional residents are added in the area by each added UCSB student (according to the UCSB Long-Term Development Report, 1974), these enrollment increases added a great deal of upward pressure on rental rates.

In 1977, the IVCC asked the County to hold public hearings on the enrollment issue during the period of rapid rent increases. But newly elected County Supervisor Bill Wallace, an I.V. resident who began his political career as a two-term member of the IVCC in the early 1970s, didn't support the request and the hearings weren't held. I.V. community leaders where shocked by Wallace's response.

By the mid-1980s, UCSB over-enrollment had become a major controversy throughout South County. Still, Wallace didn't take up this hot issue until his fourth re-election campaign in 1988.

UCSB Enrollment Levels, 1954-2006.

Year	Lower Division	Upper Division	Under-Graduate	Graduate Level 1	Graduate Level 2	Total Graduate	Total Students	Percent Graduate	Total Students
			Three Quarter Average [1]						Fall Quarter
1954-55[2]	1,008	850	1,858	25	--	25	1,883	1%	1,725
1955-56[2]	1,213	925	2,138	118	--	118	2,256	5%	2,021
1956-57			2,088	63	--	63	2,150	3%	2,220
1957-58			2,303	77	--	77	2,380	3%	2,480
1958-59			2,456	80	--	80	2,536	3%	2,722
1959-60			2,693	110	--	110	2,803	4%	2,879
1960-61			3,268	129	--	129	3,397	4%	3,511
1961-62	2,365	1,420	3,785	196	--	196	3,981	5%	4,130
1962-63	2,802	1,714	4,516	259	5	264	4,780	6%	4,865
1963-64	3,421	2,076	5,497	298	53	351	5,848	6%	5,938
1964-65	4,207	2,872	7,079	528	121	649	7,728	8%	7,879
1965-66	5,070	3,359	8,429	745	204	949	9,378	10%	9,570
1966-67	5,291	4,278	9,569	979	285	1,264	10,833	12%	11,245
1967-68	5,385	4,901	10,286	1,052	438	1,490	11,776	13%	12,201
1968-69	5,182	5,305	10,487	1,172	561	1,733	12,220	14%	12,619
1969-70	5,163	6,106	11,269	1,354	631	1,985	13,254	15%	13,733
1970-71	5,003	6,229	11,232	1,114	663	1,777	13,009	14%	13,644
1971-72	4,584	5,994	10,578	1,044	617	1,661	12,239	14%	12,916
1972-73	4,104	5,974	10,078	1,085	665	1,750	11,828	15%	12,300
1973-74	3,893	6,228	10,121	1,195	673	1,868	11,988	16%	12,526
1974-75	4,332	6,761	11,093	1,154	679	1,833	12,926	14%	13,277
1975-76	4,760	7,403	12,163	1,310	662	1,972	14,135	14%	14,584
1976-77	4,794	7,397	12,191	1,201	685	1,886	14,077	13%	14,691
1977-78	4,875	7,359	12,234	1,158	674	1,832	14,066	13%	14,588
1978-79	5,017	7,128	12,146	1,108	694	1,801	13,947	13%	14,473
1979-80	5,048	7,302	12,350	1,158	758	1,916	14,266	13%	14,785
1980-81	5,570	7,342	12,912	1,232	787	2,020	14,932	14%	15,451
New method of calculating levels of students begins in 1981-82 [3]									
1981-82	6,276	7,055	13,331	1,844	239	2,083	15,414	14%	15,711
1982-83	6,593	7,320	13,914	1,626	241	1,867	15,781	12%	16,163
1983-84	6,622	7,660	14,282	1,706	214	1,919	16,201	12%	16,753
1984-85	6,643	7,788	14,431	1,764	234	1,998	16,429	12%	16,936
1985-86	7,086	7,864	14,950	1,818	234	2,052	17,002	12%	17,415
1986-87	7,859	7,599	15,458	1,874	188	2,062	17,520	12%	18,005
1987-88	7,598	7,891	15,489	1,780	240	2,020	17,509	12%	17,879
1988-89	7,311	8,729	16,041	1,772	306	2,078	18,119	11%	18,571
1989-90	7,113	9,192	16,305	1,866	294	2,160	18,465	12%	19,082
1990-91	6,597	9,212	15,810	1,956	372	2,327	18,137	13%	18,391
1991-92	6,414	9,351	15,765	1,880	406	2,286	18,051	13%	18,519
1992-93	6,486	9,175	15,661	1,858	439	2,297	17,958	13%	18,655
1993-94	6,586	9,020	15,606	1,692	484	2,177	17,783	12%	18,581
1994-95	6,286	8,860	15,145	1,725	510	2,235	17,381	13%	17,834
1995-96	6,556	8,922	15,478	1,674	531	2,206	17,684	12%	18,224
1996-97	7,004	8,796	15,800	1,702	488	2,190	17,989	12%	18,531
1997-98	7,438	8,677	16,115	1,648	522	2,170	18,285	12%	18,940
1998-99	7,498	9,100	16,598	1,659	565	2,224	18,822	12%	19,363
1999-00	7,545	9,668	17,213	1,659	611	2,270	19,482	12%	20,056
2000-01	7,004	10,068	17,072	1,716	617	2,333	19,406	12%	19,962
2001-02	6,765	10,468	17,233	1,886	681	2,567	19,799	13%	20,373
2002-03	6,860	10,400	17,260	2,068	710	2,777	20,037	14%	20,559
2003-04	7,086	10,215	17,301	2,120	805	2,925	20,227	14%	20,847
2004-05	7,056	10,534	17,590	1,983	841	2,824	20,415	14%	21,016
2005-06	6,874	10,680	17,554	1,920	884	2,804	20,358	14%	21,016
2006-07	7,004	10,775	17,779	1,909	864	2,773	20,552	13%	21,082

[1] All numbers are 3-quarter (or 2 semester) averages unless noted otherwise.

[2] 1954-55 and 1955-56 are total students (unduplicated headcount) for the Fall and Spring Semesters.

[3] Method of counting graduate students in the G2 category changed after 1982, requiring "advancement to candidacy." Prior to 1982 the G2 classification required only 36 graduate units or a Master's degree. Minor changes were also made in the number of units required for advancement from Lower Division to Upper Division.

Note: Credential students are admitted and classified as Graduate Students at UCSB, but beginning in 1988-89 are reported by the Office of the President to the State of California as "Post-baccalaureate" students. On this table we have continued to report credential students in the Graduate Level 1 category, to remain consistent with internal UCSB reporting.

Note: Enrollment counts include students in the Education Abroad Program and all off-campus studies programs.

Also during Wallace's first term, a plan to turn Camino Pescadero Road, a major North-South artery in I.V., into a pedestrian mall was rejected by the County when Wallace's only "environmentalist" ally on the Board of Supervisors at the time, Bob Hedlund from Lompoc, failed to provide the third vote needed. The plan had been supported by over 75% of the voters in two advisory elections conducted by the IVCC and by over 95% of the residents along Camino Pescadero Road, but strongly opposed by a coalition of I.V. businesses and homeowners.

A 1988 forum on over-enrollment in UCSB's Storke Plaza. Acting Chancellor Daniel Aldrich (left), County Supervisor Bill Wallace (center) and UCSB History Professor and former County Supervisor Frank Frost address a crowd on the over-enrollment issue in the spring of 1988. First elected to the board of supervisors in 1976, Wallace did not publicly oppose UCSB over-enrollment until his 1988 reelection campaign. Wallace was a resident of Isla Vista throughout the 1970s and early '80s. Isla Vista *Free Press* photograph.

Because this was the only time Hedlund didn't vote with Wallace on an environmental issue in his four years on the board, there was much speculation in I.V. that Hedlund had taken the fall on this issue for Wallace. Hedlund later said that Wallace had not asked for his support for the Camino Pescadero Mall.

The community didn't bother to take another auto-reduction plan to the County for several more years. But in 1983, the IVCC was successful in lobbying the County to add painted bike lanes in the downtown area, over the heavy opposition of the owners of the Isla Vista Market (Verne Johnson) and the S.O.S. Liquor Store (Bob Lovgren), who complained about the loss of on-street parking spaces in front of their businesses.

The 1980s

In 1983, the County stopped its funding of the Isla Vista Community Council. The vote was 3-2 against the $10,000 allocation that the County had supplied since 1978. While Wallace voted for the request, he again was unable to secure the support of the other "environmentalist" on the-board -- this time Toru Miyoshi from Santa Maria -- for the third vote as one "pro-development" supervisor, Dwayne Holmdahl of Lompoc, voted in favor following some heavy lobbying from Isla Vista representatives.

The UCSB Administration, then under the leadership of Chancellor Robert Huttenback and Vice-

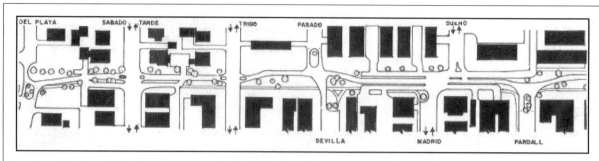

The Camino Pescadero Mall, 1975. A plan to implement a pedestrian mall along the length of a main north-south auto-traffic artery was developed by the Isla Vista Community Council and was heavily supported by local residents in an advisory election and in a door-to-door survey. The mall also included underground reservoirs to collect rainwater for Isla Vista's new parks during a period when there was a moratorium on new water hook-ups. However, the project was rejected in 1979 by the County board of supervisors. While I.V. resident and County Supervisor Bill Wallace voted for the plan, his failure to gather the vote of his strongest ally on the board, Bob Hedlund, surprised many. Hedlund later said Wallace never asked him to vote for the project. An IVCC Planning Commission drawing.

Chancellor Edward Birch, jumped on the bandwagon. Within a week of the County's decision to defund the IVCC, UCSB announced it was ending its $9,000 annual grant to the IVCC, and that they were ending all of their funding of Isla Vista service programs except police. However, Huttenback shifted the payment of the University's one-half of the Foot Patrol costs from administrative sources to student fees. That meant that all UCSB undergraduates, even those who lived in Goleta and Santa Barbara, were now paying for I.V.'s Foot Patrol.

The County, however, continued funding Isla Vista social service programs, but at a reduced level of only $60,000 per year.

So in twenty short years (1969-89), the County and UCSB Administration went back to largely ignoring Isla Vista. Meanwhile the university increased its enrollment nearly 40% while adding little student housing, causing rents to skyrocket to the point that the 1990 U.S. Census found median rents in Isla Vista to be the highest in Santa Barbara County.

By the mid-1980s, I.V.'s community-building movement had run out of steam, and in 1987, the Isla Vista Community

Robert Huttenback, UCSB chancellor from 1979 to 1986. Huttenback expanded UCSB enrollment too fast and cut off University support for Isla Vista services. He left in disgrace, but for other reasons. Isla Vista *Free Press* photograph by Keith Madigan.

Council -- once the fountainhead of that force -- went inactive.

While many of the institutions spawned during the early 1970s have remained as viable organizations, the major goal of establishing a city in Isla Vista eluded the grasp of its elected leadership.

It is to the subject of Isla Vista Cityhood that we turn next.

The Last Isla Vista Community Council, 1987. Formed in 1970, residents were elected to one-year terms annually. They lobbied the County and University in support of community positions. Isla Vista *Free Press* photograph.

Bob Lovgren (left), who was known as "Pond Scum", and Chuck "The Destructor" Eckert, once Isla Vista's most notorious absentee landlords. Over 95% of Isla Vista's dwelling units are absentee-owned. Lovgren's units are known for their plentiful supply of roaches. The Roach Inn, one of his units, is pictured below. He was once fined hundreds of thousands of dollars for evicting some 40 low-income families from one of his large

apartment complexes and lost most of his holdings as a result. Eckert created something called the Isla Vista Property Owners Association, whose members reportedly spent over $30,000 to defeat a slate of students and community activists in an election for seats on the board of directors of the Isla Vista Park District in 1992. Eckert has been at the center of opposition to any kind of city government for Isla Vista, even the inclusion of Isla Vista in a new city of Goleta in 2001. Isla Vista *Free Press* photos.

CHAPTER 5

THE SEARCH FOR A CITY

For many years, Isla Vista had a community council (the Isla Vista Community Council, IVCC), but it has never had a city council.

Cover graphic of a 1972 pamphlet produced by the Isla Vista Government Study, which presented the local government options facing Isla Vista. The pamphlet was distributed door-to-door by a team of 40 "community communicators" to brief residents on these options in advance of the November 1972 plebiscite.

In the fall of 1970, community leaders began a search for an appropriate, positive, and legal framework to promote economic and political development in Isla Vista.

The Community Action Commission, a countywide antipoverty agency, funded a study carried out by IVCC's Economic Development Commission. That study concluded that becoming a city was the best next step for the town to take.

Every person on Earth possesses the right of self-government. They receive it with their very being from the hand of Nature. The Constitutions of most of our States guarantee this right.

THOMAS JEFFERSON

Since then, the search for an appropriate form of municipal government for Isla Vista — thought by most residents to be an independent City of Isla Vista — has been a consistent goal of elected community leaders. Literally thousands of hours have been spent by IVCC members and others in the effort to get this question on the official ballot for community residents to vote on. Yet, nearly four decades after independent cityhood was first identified as a logical next step in community evolution, I.V. still has no municipal government. What's more, Isla Vistans have never had the opportunity to vote on this issue in an official election.

Why this is so makes up much of the history of Isla Vista's community development. And, it is at the center of the acrimonious relationships between the UCSB Administration and the town and between the Isla Vista Association (composed of a noisy minority of resident homeowners) and the vast majority of the community's elected leadership since 1970.

It also accounts for the town's generally inadequate urban services and excessively high rents.

The Status Quo

Isla Vista is said to be the most densely populated town west of the Mississippi River. But, unlike most urbanized areas, I.V. is unincorporated. That is, Isla Vista is neither a city nor part of another city.

Instead, most municipal services to Isla Vista (police, animal control, street and bikeway construction and repair, planning, land-use regulations, building inspection, beach cleaning, and fire protection) are provided by the County of Santa Barbara.

Water is brought to Isla Vista by a special district that I.V. shares with all of Goleta west of the City of Santa Barbara (the Goleta Water District); it is carried away by a special district covering I.V. and western Goleta (the Goleta West Sanitary District).

An independent city gained over 80%-support in that 1972 election and the IVCC began preparing an official incorporation proposal that was submitted to the Local Agency Formation Commission (LAFCO) in September 1973.

The County also owns a one-half acre park in Isla Vista and a 20-acre open space next to Isla Vista Elementary School that it bought in 1988. Both of these plots are maintained on contract by the Isla Vista Recreation and Park District, which owns and maintains the vast majority of parks in Isla Vista. The board of directors of the Isla Vista Park District is the only local government agency that is elected solely by Isla Vista residents.

For the most part, county governments and special districts are designed to provide services to rural areas, not urban communities. Although county governments have recently begun to provide some technical services (for example, fire, water and sanitation) for distinct communities within urbanized regions, cities are considered better able both to coordinate the multiple-service needs of an urbanized population and to provide the self-government framework thought to be the cornerstone of American democracy.

One of the major drawbacks to the current situation is precisely the issue of democratic representation. All County governmental decisions that affect Isla Vista are made by five members of the Board of Supervisors, only one of which is elected by Isla Vista voters. However, that seat also represents most of Goleta (also unincorporated until 2002) and the Santa Ynez Valley over the mountains. Thus, I.V. residents have only about one-third of the votes in electing one of five representatives on the Board of Supervisors. Additionally, I.V. voters makeup only about one-third of the voters in the Goleta Water District and only about 40% in the Goleta West Sanitary District. Almost all Isla Vistans vote in presidential elections, but participation in strictly local elections has dropped in Isla Vista from over 70% in the 1970s to usually less than 25% in recent years.

While Isla Vista residents make up 100% of the electorate of the I.V. Park District, on-campus and Francisco Torres residents are not allowed to vote in its elections because they are not within its boundaries.

In an attempt to improve the quality of municipal-type services the town receives from this patchwork quilt of governmental organizations, the Isla Vista Community Council tried, from 1970 until its demise in 1987, to gather a consensus of resident attitudes on various local issues and advocate for these to the actual (empowered) decision-makers. But a body that can only make recommendations to the County and University has major limitations in implementing the community's viewpoints.

A City for Isla Vistans

In 1971, the County commissioned a study of local government options facing Isla Vista and Goleta. Isla Vista activists were able to convince the Board of Supervisors to give a small share of the money allocated for the study to the IVCC, which established the Isla Vista Government Study -- an innovative examination of services and governance in Isla Vista. The Study included the hiring (at minimum wage) of 40 "community communicators" who went door-to-door several times in each neighborhood to talk with residents about these local government options.

Isla Vista Plebiscite November 1972 (4,398 voters)	
82.8%	City of Isla Vista
5.0%	Community Service District
4.5%	City of Goleta including Isla Vista
4.4%	Status Quo
3.3%	Annexing to Santa Barbara

At the end of the study period, an advisory election was held in Isla Vista -- the first of a series of "plebiscites" on local government options -- in November 1972.

The main alternatives before the voters were:

* A combined city with Goleta

* Annexing to the present City of Santa Barbara

* Establishing a Community Services District to provide a limited number of urban services

* Establishing an independent City of Isla Vista that included the UCSB campus and Francisco Torres Residence Hall, then privately owned but now belonging to UCSB.

* Maintaining the status quo

An independent city gained over 80%-support in that advisory election, and the IVCC began preparing an official incorporation proposal. It was submitted to the Local Agency Formation Commission (LAFCO) in September 1973 after literally hundreds of hours of public hearings and forums.

LAFCO is the State-mandated commission in each county, which is empowered to review the many forms of local government that communities might propose, such as establishing a new city or a special district for education, water, parks, etc., and annexations among various jurisdictions. LAFCO has final authority on whether a town can have an official election on the formation of new local government entities.

LAFCOs are composed of two members of the local County board of supervisors, two members selected from the city councils in that county, and a fifth person (the public member) chosen by those four. Two representatives from all of the special districts in the county can also be included, but this option was not pursued in Santa Barbara County until sometime in the 1990s.

The bottom line is that the members of LAFCO are not elected to this commission, although four out of five are elected to other positions and then appointed to LAFCO.

The Santa Barbara County LAFCO rejected the 1973 cityhood election request from Isla Vista on a 4-1 vote.

Annexation to Santa Barbara

Instead, LAFCO put on the ballot a plan to annex Isla Vista, Goleta, and Hope Ranch to the present City of Santa Barbara. Only Jim Slater, the County supervisor representing Isla Vista and Goleta, voted against the annexation plan.

In March 1975, area-wide voters rejected annexation 3-1; in Isla Vista, the margin was 10-1 against.

1973 Isla Vista Cityhood Proposal. Cover graphic by Al Plyley that included the statement by Thomas Jefferson quoted on the first page of this chapter.

Part of the campaign against annexation was conducted by a group of Isla Vista residents who were followers of the radical Christian theologian Thomas Merton. On the day of the election, five of these individuals sat in at a polling place in Santa Barbara as a protest against Isla Vista being included in the annexation plan over the strong protest of community residents. A judge later found them guilty of electioneering within 100 feet of a polling place, but fined them only $25.

This annexation plan never had any significant community support. It was put forward primarily by the UCSB Administration, which had opposed the plan for an independent City of Isla Vista. The local administration received a unanimous endorsement from the UC Regents to oppose a City of Isla Vista and to spend money to develop alternative municipal options for the campus and Isla Vista. Estimates at the time stated that the UCSB Administration spent at least $75,000 in support of the annexation plan; the annexation proposal was even typed in the office of a UCSB vice-chancellor.

The Second Try

After the annexation plan was defeated at the polls, the IVCC immediately called for a new advisory election in Isla Vista in order to get direction from the community as to what they should do next in the campaign to bring enhanced local government to Isla Vista. That plebiscite was held in May 1975. It was the third advisory election on local government options conducted in Isla Vista.

This plebiscite produced another landslide favoring the independent incorporation of I.V. Dutifully, the IVCC prepared and submitted another request to the Santa Barbara County LAFCO in late 1975.

If LAFCO had approved the request for an election on I.V. cityhood and if Isla Vista voters had approved it, the new City of Isla Vista would have been created on July 4th, 1976 — the 200th anniversary of the Declaration of Independence.

Literally hundreds of Isla Vista residents attended the LAFCO hearings to speak in favor of the proposal. The major opposition remained some I.V. homeowners, business owners, and landlords, but not a majority of any of these interests. And, of course, the UCSB Administration.

Poster for the May 1975 Plebiscite. Graphic design by Mike Gold.

During this second cityhood campaign, the UCSB Administration hired a local consulting firm that lied for them, writing that it was likely the City of Isla Vista would have to have its own fire department and couldn't afford it. The truth was that Isla Vista was part of a county fire services district that the community would have to vote itself out of, which it was most unlikely do. Based on this false information, the consultant found the proposed city to not be "financially feasible."

Of course, this fire department issue was also raised by the UCSB Administration to remind everyone of the unruly crowds that in 1970 burned the Bank of America to the ground. Just because they run a great university doesn't mean they have to play fair!

In early 1976, the UCSB Administration again asked the UC Regents to oppose I.V. cityhood because, based on their consultant's report, it supposedly wasn't "financially feasible". While the Regents did oppose Isla Vistans having an election on forming a city, their vote was far from unanimous; at least five

Regents stood in favor of the community's position.

During the discussion Regent Leo McCarthy, then speaker of the State Assembly and later the lieutenant governor, stated: "I've traveled all over this state and I have seldom found the kind of commitment to community that the people of Isla Vista have shown. I don't believe that it is in the best interests of the University to be against this." Also, Regents Norton Simon, Fred Dutton, and William Mattson Roth made stirring statements in support of cityhood for Isla Vista.

However, perhaps the most memorable comment was made by Regent Glenn Campbell, head of the ultraconservative Hoover Institute for the Study of War at Stanford University, who picked up on the talking point handed out by the UCSB Administration:

"What if there's another conflagration in Isla Vista," he asked shrilly. "We couldn't count on your fire department to put it out!"

The Speaker of the California State Assembly Leo McCarthy (left) on a bicycle tour of Isla Vista in 1976. McCarthy's tour was guided by IVCC Rep. Cindy Wachter and IVCC staffer Carmen Lodise. As a member of the UC Regents, McCarthy strongly endorsed the City of Isla Vista. He later became California's lieutenant governor. Goleta *Today* photo by Wendy Thermos.

The Regents' final position was to oppose I.V. cityhood in favor of including the UCSB campus in the largest city government possible, most likely a combined city with Goleta.

During these discussions, the IVCC had asked the Regents to simply remain neutral, since what form of local government Isla Vista (including the UCSB campus) might have was hardly an issue of statewide importance.

At the end of the day, LAFCO again rejected the request for Isla Vista residents to vote on establishing a City of Isla Vista, bottomlining it that the proposed city was not "financially feasible." However, Isla Vista representatives at the time felt that the real reasons were political, because Isla Vista looked as good on paper as any other city in the county. In addition, on both occasions the membership of LAFCO was 4-1 Republicans at a time Democratic voter registration in I.V. was above 80%; Jim Slater was again Isla Vista's lone supporter and LAFCO's sole Democrat.

Soon after the second cityhood proposal was shot down, Slater was elected to a judgeship representing Isla Vista, Goleta, and Santa Barbara. Although he won only 11 precincts outside of Isla Vista, his greater than 90%-support in Isla Vista was enough to give him the election by a handful of votes.

Financial Feasibility

That a City of Isla Vista is not "financially feasible" has been repeated so many times that even many of cityhood's most ardent supporters have come to accept it. Although it is a false issue on several counts, it has been an effective guise keeping Isla Vista cityhood off the official ballot.

It is false because it implies that a proposed city, which on paper has a shortfall in projected revenues over projected expenditures, should – on face value — be disqualified from going before the voters.

It was also false because LAFCOs at that time had no authority to use "financial feasibility" as criteria in judging whether a proposal could be placed on the ballot. In fact, LAFCO only had responsibility to make certain any revenue increase thought to be necessary for a balanced budget was accurately stated in the ballot measure to be placed before voters.

Finally, it was false because it was based on the assumption that LAFCO has the authority to

1975 Isla Vista Incorporation Proposal. Cover graphic by Mike Gold, based on a concept by Arthur Longoria.

establish what level of services the proposed city would have, and therefore how much total expenditures would be. In fact, only the first city council of the proposed city would establish the actual expenditure levels for the city, not LAFCO. And it was the proponents of cityhood who represented that first city council in LAFCO deliberations, not LAFCO staff.

So how could "financial feasibility" have become such a huge roadblock to Isla Vista becoming a city?

At the time, estimating expected revenues for proposed cities was pretty straightforward. Fundamentally total revenue depended on the number of registered voters, the total assessed valuation of property, and the number of motor vehicles registered within the boundaries of the proposed city.

However, there's a real art to estimating what total expenditures might be because they depend on both salary and benefit levels the city council decides to pay and how many workers will be needed to perform the duties the council requests.

The proponents of the City of Isla Vista used current salaries and service levels provided by the County of Santa Barbara to generate estimated expenditures. What better standard could there be? Or should there be? Using these numbers for expenditures and revenues, the proposed city had a significant budget surplus well into the future.

However, in his assessment of the proposal LAFCO staff included two more police officers than the proponents had. He did this, he said, because the sheriff had asked for two more positions during the previous County budget hearings. Even though the elected board of supervisors had rejected the request, this bureaucrat's opinion held for LAFCO members. LAFCO staff also adopted the UCSB-invented position that the proposed City of Isla Vista would be required to have its own fire department at a major extra cost, even though the county fire chief testified that this would not be needed and wasn't recommended. With these padded expenditures, the proposed city would be running a significant deficit.

The proponents of the City of Isla Vista used current salaries and service levels provided by the County of Santa Barbara to generate estimated expenditures. What better standard could there be?

But this wasn't enough. A recent court order required LAFCOs to do an environmental impact report on all proposals before it. Adopting the inflated expenditure estimates presented by the UCSB Administration's consultant, LAFCO staff said the proposed City of Isla Vista would have an unmitigatable negative impact on the environment because it could not afford to provide a necessary level of service.

But the staff report went further, suggesting that the only way for the proposed city to cover this alleged deficit would be to raise property taxes. Raising property taxes, it said, would be so onerous that many apartment owners would have to walk away from their properties and Isla Vista would degenerate into a slum. This was another unmitigatable negative environmental impact, in staff's opinion.

This image played right into the biases of the four Republicans on LAFCO, and all four put the frosting on this cake by conjecturing at one point or another that an Isla Vista City Council would most likely impose rent controls, which would also hasten the transformation of a student ghetto into a slum.

However, Isla Vista is not an ordinary town because 96% of its residents are renters. Since all property owners have to pay property taxes, there is no competitive disadvantage to individual landlords when they are increased. Therefore, an increase in the tax on property is immediately passed on to tenants in higher rents. And, in this writer's 30 years of involvement in Isla Vista, no I.V. landlord has ever gone broke, except those who built or bought too close to the bluff.

This argument, however, was too abstract for Republicans.

Supposedly shaky finances, the specter of rent control, and the failure of cityhood proponents to get the masters of their company town – the UCSB Administration – to sign on to the project were all too much for the four Republicans. UCSB, after all, was by far the county's biggest employer and if there's anything Republicans can viscerally relate to it is economic power. As noted, the final vote was 4-1 against, with only County Supervisor Jim Slater raising his hand in favor.

In their summary statements, all four Republicans said they voted against the proposal because the City of Isla Vista wasn't "financially feasible" and that label has stuck through the years.

The Dos Pueblos Years

After the second attempt for an Isla Vista cityhood election was killed by LAFCO, another proposal was prepared by the IVCC in 1978, but it wasn't submitted. A strong push for a combined city of Isla Vista and Goleta by newly elected County Supervisor Bill Wallace accounted for the inaction.

Following a suggestion from Isla Vista, Wallace called his proposed city "Dos Pueblos", Spanish for "two towns". This was in deference to the well-known differences between the middle-class homeowners in Goleta and the young renters in Isla Vista. But the name had some historical value, too, in that most of the area proposed to be a city was the Dos Pueblos Land Grant in the Mexican Period. It is also the name of the high school that serves both towns.

Although LAFCO agreed to be put this plan on the ballot, Wallace withdrew it without a citizen-vote because of some conditions not to his liking that were imposed by the rest of the County supervisors.

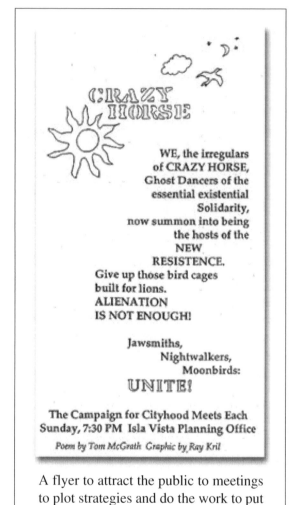

CRAZY HORSE

WE, the irregulars of CRAZY HORSE, Ghost Dancers of the essential existential Solidarity, now summon into being the hosts of the NEW RESISTENCE. Give up those bird cages built for lions. ALIENATION IS NOT ENOUGH!

Jawsmiths, Nightwalkers, Moonbirds: UNITE!

The Campaign for Cityhood Meets Each Sunday, 7:30 PM Isla Vista Planning Office

Poem by Tom McGrath Graphic by Ray Kril

A flyer to attract the public to meetings to plot strategies and do the work to put cityhood on the ballot. About 1977. Poem by Tom McGrath. Graphic by Ray Kril.

For several years, the movement to bring city government to Isla Vista languished. It returned, however, with a vengeance as the result of the November 1982 IVCC election and plebiscite on local government options.

Before we leave the 1970s, however, there are a few more stories to tell.

CHAPTER 6

THE ISLA VISTA PARK DISTRICT

Isla Vista residents established the Isla Vista Recreation and Park District in a 1972 election held on Halloween Day, before the serious partying started around sunset.

At the time, there was only one park in Isla Vista – the County's Ocean View Park, better known as "Dog Shit Park", on Del Playa Dr. at Camino Corto Rd.

In 1974, a State grant bought and built Children's Park along Picasso Rd. at Camino Del Sur Rd., and a federal grant was secured that built Anisq'Oyo Park in 1975-76 on what used to be the middle of the 6500 block of Madrid Rd.

But things got serious in 1975, when I.V. voters approved a $1.15 bond measure that permitted the purchase of 14 other parklands, including:

- Window-to-the-Sea Park on Del Playa Drive

- Sueño Park

- Trigo/Pasado Park

- Greek Park on Embarcadero del Norte Road

- Camino Pescadero Park on Del Playa Drive

- People's Park next to UCSB's Embarcadero Hall

- Pardall Gardens

- Tipi Village in the 6700 block of Sueño Rd.

- Sueño Orchard across the street from Tipi Village

- Estero Community Gardens

- Litle Acorn Park at the meeting of the three Embarcaderos

Mikey Jett coming off the slide in Isla Vista's Children's Park along Picasso Rd. at Camino Del Sur Rd. It was purchased and built in 1974 with the first in a series of State park bonds. Children's Park was the first park owned by the Isla Vista Park District. 1987 photograph by the Isla Vista *Free Press.*

- an expansion of the County's Ocean View Park on Del Playa Drive

- Estero Park along Estero Road from Camino del Sur Rd. to Camino Corto Road

- Del Sol Vernal Pool Preserve

In recent years, the County's Isla Vista Redevelopment Agency has purchased important lots along the Del Playa bluff top and Santa Barbara County purchased and gave to the Park District the 20-acre open space adjacent to Isla Vista Elementary School.

The Park District now owns or maintains 25 parks in Isla Vista totaling 57 acres. But it was a struggle getting to this point.

In the 1970s and most of the '80s, the region had a severe water shortage, which meant Isla Vista's new parks didn't have water to keep them green. For years many community-owned parcels remained scruffy lots (technically called "open space") that were only minimally maintained.

Today, there is no water shortage and all parklands are green and cheerful. However, almost every vacant lot not owned by the community has been developed.

If not for the foresight of Isla Vista voters to preserve open space through the years, there would still be only one park in this crowded campus town.

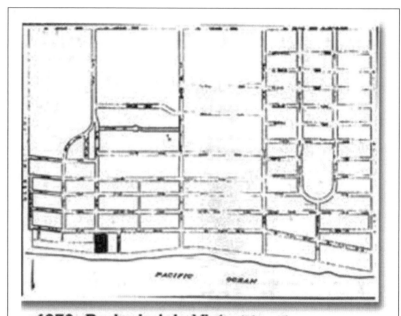

1970: Parks in Isla Vista (above).
1995: Parks in Isla Vista (below).

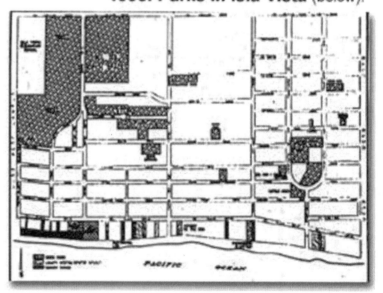

Graphic from <u>IMAGES of the Isla Vista Medical Clinic, 1970-95</u> (1995) written by Carmen Lodise in commemoration of the I.V. Clinic's 25th Anniversary.

The Stage and Amphitheater in Anisq'Oyo Park.
It may not look like much when the stage is empty, but on most weekend afternoons it holds nearly 1,000 people, including a lot of dancers. Isla Vista *Free Press* photos by Keith Madigan.

"Anisq'Oyo" is the Chumash Indian name for the Isla Vista mesa that contains the town and the UCSB campus. The park was built with a federal urban renewal grant following the civil disturbances of 1969-70. UC Regent Norton Simon personally contributed $69,500 to the project.

Isla Vista Festivals in Anisq'Oyo Park.

For years, there has been a Fall and a Spring Festival in Anisq'Oyo Park. There also have been other traditional events, such as the annual Jugglers' Festival held the first weekend in April and attracting jugglers from up and down the West Coast and beyond.

Then there's Bob Marley's Birthday Bash in February and the old Joint Rolling Contests (see Chapter 8). All such festivals feature free live music and lots of dancing. Isla Vista *Free Press* photographs.

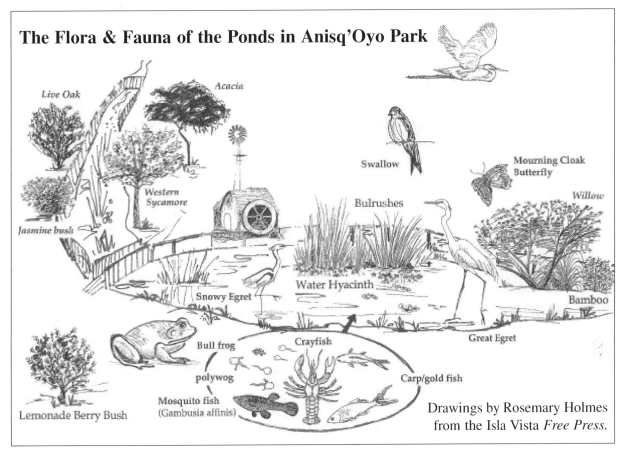

The Flora & Fauna of the Ponds in Anisq'Oyo Park

Live Oak

Acacia

Western Sycamore

Jasmine bush

Swallow

Mourning Cloak Butterfly

Willow

Bulrushes

Snowy Egret

Water Hyacinth

Great Egret

Bamboo

Bull frog

Crayfish

polywog

Mosquito fish (Gambusia affinis)

Carp/gold fish

Lemonade Berry Bush

Drawings by Rosemary Holmes from the Isla Vista *Free Press*.

The ponds in Anisq'Oyo Park were intended to collect rainfall to irrigate the park, because the park was built in the 1970s when there was no public water supply. The dirt removed to hold the ponds was used to build the amphitheater. The picture (above) of one of the ponds was the front cover of an issue of the Isla Vista *Free Press* in 1988.

I.V. Park District grounds workers in the late 1980s. Left to right: Ramon Alvarez, Tim O'Day, Alice Chouinard, Eddie Jordon. I.V. *Free Press*.

Bob Henderson: The Visionary Teacher

In what was perhaps its most magnanimous gesture during the early 1970s, the UCSB Administration loaned its campus planner to the Isla Vista Community Council's planning department for two years, 1972-74.

During his tenure with IVCC, John Robert "Bob" Henderson taught dozens of students and other residents basic land-use planning and how these tools could apply in Isla Vista. He also assisted in the development of a community plan, which lead to literally hundreds of hours of discussions on how to down-zone the town from 44,000 in a half-square-mile to 24,000 residents, establish a network of bikelanes, and initiate mini-bus routes connecting the town to the campus and to Goleta and Santa Barbara (most of it accomplished). And the vision of a car-free Isla Vista. All of this and more was published in 1973 as Recommendations for Isla Vista Planning (see cover below). And he made everyone involved in the process feel like they had invented the new plans themselves.

But the icing on the cake was his design of Anisq'Oyo Park. No public water supply? Dig deep ponds to catch the winter rains. What to do with the dirt? Use it to build an amphitheater where free music has played on most weekends for over 30 years.

Thanks, Bob.

Former UCSB Campus Planner Bob Henderson shown here during a visit to Isla Vista in 1988. Isla Vista *Free Press* photograph.

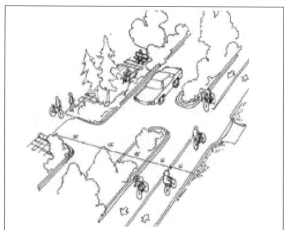

A drawing of what bikelanes could be. From Recommendations for Isla Vista Planning (1973).

Isla Vista Park District Special Projects

Greek Park, Embarcadero del Norte at Segovia Rd. (right). As a means to draw the fraternities and sororities into the community, the Park District purchased this large lot, which has nearly a dozen Greek houses within a block. The park, which contains well-used basketball and volleyball courts, is maintained by the Greeks. Isla Vista *Free Press* photographs.

items and some people take them home. Originally sited at the south end of the Isla Vista Medical Clinic building, it was moved to the front yard of the Park District offices (above) when the clinic was remodeled in the late 1980s. The Park District has cut back the size of the Free Box recently (below).

The Free Box, an Isla Vista tradition since the late 1960s, has been maintained by the Park District in recent years. Some people drop off

Sueño Park (above) is one of several pocket parks with picnic tables.

For many years, the Park District ran a program in which residents, who had traffic infractions and other misdemeanors, could sweep I.V. streets (right) for "community service" instead of paying cash fines.

Del Sol Park and Vernal Pool Preserve

One of Isla Vista's parks is very special. Purchased for $104,000 in 1978 from the $1.15-million bond approved by I.V. voters in 1975, it has several vernal pools. With a State grant, this 12-acre parcel became the first vernal pool preserve in California.

Isla Vista's Del Sol Park and Vernal Pool Preserve at Camino Corto and El Colegio roads, as seen from the top floor of Francisco Torres Residence Hall. I.V. *Free Press* photos.

Vernal pools are seasonally flooded depressions found on ancient soils with an impermeable layer such as a hardpan, claypan, or volcanic basalt. The impermeable layer allows the pools to retain water much longer then the surrounding uplands; nonetheless, the pools are shallow enough to dry up each season. Only plants and animals that are adapted to this cycle of wetting and drying can survive in vernal pools over time.

As winter rains fill the pools, freshwater invertebrates, crustaceans, and amphibians emerge. Vernal pool plants sprout underwater, some using special floating leaves and air-filled stems to stay afloat. In spring, flowering plants produce brightly-colored concentric rings of flowers that vernal pools are famous for. Insects and crustaceans produce cysts and eggs, and plants produce seeds that are buried in the muddy pool bottom, which protects them from the hot, dry summer. By late summer, amphibians have dug deep into the soils and gone dormant, awaiting the next rainy season. In this phase, vernal pools are really "banks" full of resting seeds, cysts, and eggs that can survive through summer, and even extended droughts, until the onset of rains begin the life cycle anew. Source: http://www.vernalpools.org/

I.V. Park District, State and County officials at the ground-breaking ceremony in 1978. This was the first vernal pool preserve in California. To see how it was developed, go to: http://www.sinauer.com/groom/article.php?id=13

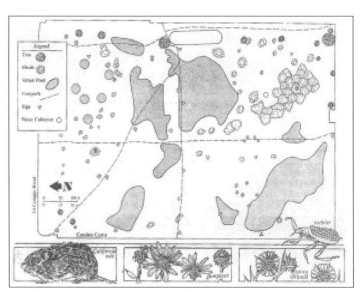

In its early days, the Isla Vista Park District had offices at 966C Embarcadero del Mar, more-or-less across the street from where it is today. But in the late 1970s, it moved to 889 Camino del Sur, a two-story structure (pictured right) next to the Red Barn, both of which were purchased with the $1.15-million Park Bond of 1975. In 1988, the District moved into its present location, a refurbished gasoline station at 961 Embarcadero del Mar (below left).

There would not have been an Isla Vista Park District without the early work of attorney Tom Stone. At the time, property owners, on a $1/1 vote according to the assessed valuation of their property, could veto putting on the ballot a measure to form a new local government entity (special district, community services district, municipality, etc.). I.V. property owners, unconcerned that I.V.'s 15,000 people were living in a half-square mile that only

had one park, and figuring that a park district would cost them profits because it ran on property taxes, were able to round up a 50.55% opposition to the formation of a park district.

Working with community volunteers, Tom Stone (below) was able to disqualify enough of the signatures on the opposition petition (some were no longer

owners of I.V. property, some were not legal representatives of the property they voted on, etc.) to push the opposition under 50%. The formation of the district went on the ballot Oct. 31, 1972 and passed overwhelmingly. Stone has been the Park District's attorney for most of the years since then. Thanks, Tom.

Note: the property owner veto over local government formation options was thrown out by the California Supreme Court a few weeks after the Park District went on the ballot.

CHAPTER 7

TIPI VILLAGE

People began living in tipis in Isla Vista in the 1960s.

When I arrived in Isla Vista in 1972, there were at least 25 tipis sprinkled throughout the town. Many were in backyards, but most were in vacant lots owned by people who were such distant absentee-owners that they never noticed them. Of course, if the owner happened to visit his property and kick off the squatter, it was easy enough to pick up the structure and move it to another vacant lot -- after all, Indians had lived like this for centuries.

There was even a store in Isla Vista -- New World Resources -- that sold tipis. A new one cost about $400, as I remember. For the most part these tipi-dwellers were left alone, seldom bothered by either the police or County government officials.

Tipi Village

In the late 1970s, however, the practice suddenly mushroomed.

Almost overnight, there were well over sixty tipis around town, with 21 of them concentrated on one lot in the 6700 block of Sueño Road. Most people attribute this dramatic increase in the number of tipi dwellers to the huge rent increases that began in 1975, which is when enrollment at UCSB began to skyrocket. Enrollment at UCSB had been under 12,500 in 1972, but it jumped an average of 1,000 a year in the mid-'70s. Although it settled back some after that, fall enrollment was over 16,000 by 1982. See page 64. Vacancy signs became an endangered species around Isla Vista and rents saw double-digit increases annually throughout the period.

A graphic by Jade, a resident of Tipi Village, on a poster supporting Villagers. See the next page for the words of Holly Near quoted on the face of the tipi.

But the concentration of so many tipis on a cypress-lined lot that had become known as Tipi Village became too much for government officials to overlook. In 1979, the board of directors of the Isla Vista Sanitary District (renamed the Goleta West Sanitary District in the early 1990s as part of an Isla Vista bashing scheme) voted unanimously to ask the sheriff to evict the dwellers from Tipi Village, supposedly because there were no official toilets on the property. This action was taken despite the directors having been informed that the Villagers were permitted to use the toilets next door to the property at the I.V. Park District's then-offices.

The Villagers actually had been paying rent on this property for a number of years. The owner was an elderly woman who was confined to a rest home. Although the rent was a modest amount, she was happy to receive some return on this property that she couldn't build on because of the water hook-up moratorium imposed by area voters in 1973.

The life-style in the Village was wholly organic, with Villagers growing their food without benefit of pesticides in community gardens established by the I.V. Park District along Estero Road, contiguous on the north to the Village. These gardens still exist.

> **hang in there**
>
> the seeds don't get in the ground
>
> if you just sit and think about the
>
> harvest. you got to go out and plant
>
> 'em. and do it is with change. it's
>
> like a summer day to dream of world peace,
>
> sexual and racial equality, ageless under-
>
> standing – but it we don't go out and plant
>
> 'em, there will be no harvest. So to all you
>
> farmers, hang in there. it's going to be a
>
> long spring.
>
> holly near

Park District Buys Tipi Village

A couple of weeks before the I.V. San. Board voted to evict the Villagers, the I.V. Park District purchased the property on which the Village was located. Almost immediately, I.V. Park District staff submitted a plan to the County to establish an official camp ground at the Tipi Village site utilizing chemical toilets. Such a land-use designation would have saved Tipi Village -- at least until its inhabitants had changed their life-styles and moved away under their own volition.

A group of Isla Vista activists and Village residents had attended the I.V. San. Board meeting at which the board issued its eviction notice, asking the directors to not take any action until the County had decided on the Park District's campsite plan. But, the San. District directors turned a deaf ear to this request and voted unanimously to seek the eviction immediately.

Many I.V. residents became indignant at this treatment from the sanitary district board, especially since Isla Vistans represented 40% of the voters in the district. Even if most Isla Vistans weren't interested in living the tipi-life-style themselves, they did feel that this was a valued experiment in alternative living.

Plus, the Park District was taking over the property and trying to make a legal, up-to-code operation out of what had been an illegal situation for years.

About the same time, an advisory election was conducted by the Isla Vista Community Council on the question of Tipi Village. Over 70% of the 1,700 people voting in the election favored the Park District's plan to set up a campsite to save Tipi Village.

Recall!

At a well-attended community meeting called by Tipi Villagers, it was decided to launch a recall campaign against the I.V. San. Board for their arrogance in not letting the County permit-process go to its conclusion.

Tipi Village Park. This cypress-lined park in the 6700 block of Sueño Road once held a village of tipi dwellers. Attempts by the Isla Vista Park District to legalize the village were unsuccessful.

The recall campaign was incredibly popular. People were chasing petition carriers down the street to get their signatures on it! "Save Tipi Village -- Sign the Recall Petition" banners went up all over town. Buttons depicting a toilet seat and saying "Get Your Shit Together -- Citizens for Responsible Sanitary Policies" were sold out as soon as they were hand-stamped. It was so easy to get signatures that the campaign ran out of petitions for a couple of days. Over half of the 3,200 signatures to establish a recall election for three of the five directors were collected within 10 days.

But the campaign was also very divisive in Isla Vista. Some people were outraged that the Villagers could live in situations paying so little rent, while others hated the "hippie" life-style of the Villagers. A petition containing the signatures of over 2,000 people had been gathered opposing Tipi Village in the few weeks preceding the San. District's decision. Most of these signatures, however, were from Goleta residents, not Isla Vistans; some were even from the Santa Ynez Valley.

The Gambit

In an attempt to diminish these intra-community wars, the leaders of the recall campaign took a calculated risk. They walked into the next meeting of the I.V. San. Board and gave the petitions gathered-to-date, which contained roughly 1,600 signatures, to the board of directors and announced they were calling off the recall campaign. They then asked the board to reconsider their decision from two weeks earlier to have the sheriff immediately evict the Villagers and to wait the 3-4 months that it would take the County to decide on the Park District's campsite plan.

The I.V. San Board quickly voted unanimously to call off their eviction effort. Needless to say, there were visible sighs of relief on both sides of the issue.

Supes Reject Campsite

A few months later, the Board of Supervisors voted 4-1 against the rezoning of Tipi Village into a campsite. The most strident voices at the hearing against the campsite were families from Isla Vista's St. Athanasius (Evangelical Orthodox) Church (see Chapter 12) and a couple of people who lived near the Village. But, as the UCSB *Daily Nexus* reported at the time, "the final blow against the Village was organized, researched, and carried out by the Evangelical Orthodox Church" (Oct. 17, 1979, page 1).

The *Daily Nexus* also reported that the testimony against the Tipi Villagers was "emotional, although not strictly to the point," and "gave the impression" that the Villagers were "being accused of being drunken, disease-carrying rapists."

Traditional prejudices against Isla Vista also played a part. Supervisor David Yeager (from the wealthy enclave of Montecito) said in voting against the campsite plan that, "There were already too many transients in Isla Vista!"

Estero Community Gardens lie in the 6700 block of Estero Road. It's part of a 6.3-acre park that abuts Tipi Village Park. The gardens were very popular among the Cambodian and Hmong refugees of the Vietnam War who settled in Isla Vista in the late 1970s.

Keeping to their promise to live by the results of the Supervisor's decision, the Villagers abandoned Tipi Village within a few days. Before they left, they held a dinner party for all of the people who had helped in the effort to save the Village; it was one of the warmest and saddest events I ever attended in Isla Vista.

Bill Wallace, who still lived in Isla Vista at that time, was the only County supervisor to vote in favor of the campsite option. A few months later, when he was running for reelection, hand-painted signs appeared around Isla Vista urging people to "Vote No on Tipi Bill."

He won re-election handily.

CHAPTER 8

THE JOINT ROLLING CONTESTS

Between 1976 and 1981, each Isla Vista Fall and Spring Festival featured a Joint Rolling Contest. I was the Master of Ceremonies, but only because I organized the event.

Actually, the event featured three contests. One was for best ("The Most Primo") joint, a second for the biggest joint (with a two-paper limit), and the third for the fastest joint roller.

The fastest contest required several heats with six rollers in each heat. The winner of each heat would then enter a runoff contest to determine the overall winner. For some reason, women usually won this contest.

Fantastic Prizes

Prizes were awarded to the three winners: usually a fine bong, or maybe an antler pipe, a poster, etc. The prizes were always donated by Bamboo Brothers, a great head shop located at the corner of Pardall and Embarcadero del Mar. The actual winning joints were posted on a plaque at Bamboo Brothers until the next contest, which greatly increased the prestige of the winners.

As the M.C., I got to select the judges. There were always three

Joint Rolling Contests were held each Fall and Spring Festival in Isla Vista's Anisq'Oyo Park for many years in the late 1970s and early 1980s. Poster graphic by Carmen Lodise, with a little help from Albrect Durer and Mike Gold.

90

judges, the odd number being necessary to break ties, especially in the Most Primo Joint category.

County Supervisor Jim Slater (left-center, top) was one of three judges in the first Isla Vista Joint Rolling Contest held during the Fall Festival in Anisq'Oyo Park, September 1976. Santa Barbara *News-Press* photograph.

As you can imagine, this was a very difficult judgment to make.

Celebrity Judges

Actually, who the judges were was one of the biggest hits of the event. I usually chose people who were running for office, often candidates for municipal or superior court judge -- how better to test their qualifications to be a judge. Jim Slater and his opponent for Municipal Court Judge, Alice Merenbach, plus Floyd Dodson, a sitting superior court judge running for re-election, were the first three celebrity judges.

Pictures of Slater being a contest judge were published in the UCSB *Daily NEXUS*. A supporter of Isla Vista Cityhood as a member of the Local Agency Formation Commission (LAFCO) in both 1973 and 1976, the organization in charge of accepting or rejecting requests for communities to vote on cityhood, Slater won only 11 precincts in Santa Barbara and Goleta in his campaign for a judgeship. But he had the highest vote total overall because he received more than 90% of the vote in Isla Vista. However, when a picture of Dodson as a contest judge appeared on the front page of the Santa Barbara *News-Press*, he became the first superior court judge in California history to fail to be reelected.

Other contest judges through the years included County Supervisor Bill Wallace, District Attorney Stan Roden, and Harvey Clement, director of CETA job training programs for the County at the time CETA was spending over $2 million a year in Isla Vista on training jobs. Plus, almost all of the candidates for the Goleta Water Board during those years found it necessary to make an appearance as a "judge" in this event.

We even once had a member of the Foot Patrol -- in uniform -- as a judge. Actually, that contest took place during his last hour as a member of the Foot Patrol, so he didn't get into trouble.

Bob Brandts, owner of a notorious tavern in Goleta, The English Department, was also a judge one year. However, this didn't turn out too well. When it became obvious that he was throwing the Most Primo Joint contest to an attractive female roller, there were a lot of boos. He wasn't invited back.

Isla Vista Green

What did we use as filler in these joints? Parsley; we called it "Isla Vista Green."

While the contests were wildly popular for several years, it became obvious in the early 1980s that interest was waning when only a dozen people showed up for the "Fastest Joint Roller" contest in 1981.

County Supervisor Jim Slater goofing off as a judge in the first Isla Vista Joint Rolling Contest, September 1976. As a supervisor, Slater represented Isla Vista and Goleta and is remembered as one of the area's first elected environmentalists. He also supported Isla Vista Cityhood as a member of LAFCO. At the time he was judging the Joint Rolling Contest, he was running for a municipal court judgeship, which he won largely because of the greater-than-90% vote he received in Isla Vista. UCSB *Daily Nexus* photo.

Superior Court Judge Floyd Dodson pictured as one of three judges in the first Isla Vista Joint Rolling Contest, September 1976. This photo of Dodson appeared on the front page of the Santa Barbara *News-Press*. His son, Walter, maintains that the judge always thought that this picture was the main reason he became the first superior court judge in California history to lose a re-election bid. Santa Barbara *News-Press* photograph.

Since the original event was a way for all of us to laugh both at ourselves and society, when the crowds dwindled I figured it had become passe. Times had changed.

In the mid-'80s, people from the St. Athanasius Church (see Chapter 12) complained to LAFCO that Isla Vistans shouldn't be allowed to vote on having an independent city because we did things like have joint rolling contests, "which were both illegal and immoral."

Some people just don't have a sense of humor.

PS I understand the contest has been resurrected in recent years.

CHAPTER 9

THE PEOPLE IN THE GREEN AREA

Isla Vista homeowner Bruce Murdock stood before the Local Agency Formation Commission (LAFCO) on a fall day in 1976. The map of Isla Vista he was showing the Commission had Isla Vista's West End colored red, while the rest of the town was colored green.

After a short presentation, he cried out: "You've got to save us from the people in the Green Area!"

The battle between the 50 or so resident-homeowners who make up the membership of the Isla Vista Association (IVA) and the community's elected leadership has raged almost since the IVA's formation in 1968.

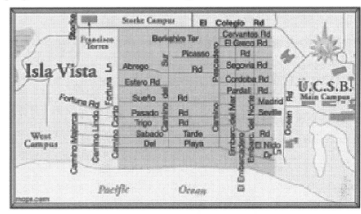

In this map of Isla Vista, the darkened area is what the R-1 presenter to LAFCO called "the Green Area." The map was created by Bryan Corant, a 1997 UCSB graduate.

The IVA has opposed all three attempts by Isla Vista residents to secure an election on becoming a city (1973, 1975, and 1984), the first Park Bond in 1974 (which failed 66-34% at the ballot — 66.7% is required for passage), the second $1.15 million Park Bond in 1975 (which passed 67-33%), the 1988 $500,000 Park Bond (which failed 64-36%), and the $10-per-household tax for park services (which passed 71-39%) in 1984.

The IVA also favored the ban on open containers of alcohol on the street enacted by the County in 1987 and the inclusion of Isla Vista in a City of Goleta, which was defeated by area voters 2-1 in November 1987.

But no political campaign has so indicated the alienation of Isla Vista's homeowners from the mainstream of political life in Isla Vista, as did the 1976 attempt by these people to secede from the Isla Vista. Recreation and Park District. What made this effort even more painful was that the Park District, formed in 1972, was one of the few community projects that most IVA members supported at the time.

The Isla Vista Association

Most members of the IVA are resident-property owners living at the West End of town in the area zoned R-1 for single-family homes. Although students and tenants are eligible to join the IVA, longtime

IVA leader Les Baird told a 1985 IVA meeting that, "We've never had more than a half dozen student members in the IVA since we started."

Although a majority of R-1 residents are usually renters, the IVA leadership has convinced most outside authorities that they are the "authentic" representatives of that end of town. Further, these same outside authorities view the IVA as the representatives of the "permanent" residents of Isla Vista, as opposed to either the transient students who make up the majority of the rest of Isla Vista or the tenants who make up 96% of all of Isla Vista.

Property Rights & LAFCO as the Judge

It is illegal to deny political rights to non-property owners, just as it is to deny civil rights to people because of their ethnicity.

> *It is illegal to deny political rights to non-property owners, just as it is to deny civil rights to people because of their ethnicity. But in the real world, ethnic minorities are discriminated against and outside political authorities weigh the opinions of resident-property owners greater than they do tenants in matters relating to Isla Vista.*

Bruce Murdock, an R-1 home-owner, who served on the Isla Vista Park Board 1976-80 and 1988-96. Despite warning LAFCO that the tenant-supported Park Board was going to "make R-1 homeowners an endangered species", Murdoch still lives in Isla Vista and is running again for the Park Board in 2008. Isla Vista *Free Press* photo.

But in the real world, ethnic minorities are discriminated against and outside political authorities weigh the opinions of resident-property owners greater than they do tenants in matters relating to Isla Vista.

This bias has assisted the IVA leadership in all of their battles against the majority-residents of I.V., and the IVA leadership was counting on this bias when they asked the County's Local Agency Formation Commission (LAFCO) to detach the R-1 area of Isla Vista from the boundaries of the Park District.

The LAFCO membership at the time was quite familiar with the Isla Vista situation, because most of them had been on the Commission when it turned down Isla Vista's second cityhood election petition just a few months before the IVA's detachment request.

County Assessor's Role

Besides their alienation from the majority tenants of Isla Vista, the homeowners were angry because they were being forced to pay more property taxes than the rest of town due to the unbelievable unfairness of the County Assessor. Although the standard practice of that pre-Prop. 13 era was to reevaluate properties every four years for purposes of assessing property taxes, Isla Vista had not been re-assessed for seven years. Some people speculated that the County Assessor had Isla Vista's re-assessment intentionally delayed in order to make the property tax base of the proposed City of Isla Vista look low during the 1976 LAFCO proceedings. In those times, cities depended a great deal more on property taxes than they do today.

But shortly after the second I.V. cityhood election request was turned down by LAFCO, the County Assessor announced that the R-1 section of Isla Vista would be re-assessed for that year's taxpaying purposes, but that the rest of I.V. would not be re-assessed until at least a year later. Because it had been seven years since the previous assessment, property taxes were going to increase at least 50% in the R-1. In addition, because the 1975 Park Bond had passed in the previous November's election, it meant that R-1 property owners

> *"These people in the Green Area are trying to tax us out of town."*
>
> BRUCE MURDOCH
> R-1 Homeowner

would be paying two or three times the amount for these bonds for the first year than would similar property owners elsewhere in town.

It was all too galling to the IVA leaders. After all, they had been vehemently opposed to the passage of the bonds and to the election on a city, but now they were being forced to pay more for these bonds than if the city had been established.

The IVA wanted out of the Park District!

I.V. Home Owners Extinct?

In making the presentation to LAFCO, IVA leader Bruce Murdock displayed a map showing the R-1 section of the Park District in red, and the balance of Isla Vista in green.

"These people in the Green Area are trying to tax us out of town," he proclaimed to loud applause from his supporters.

"It's not the exotic bugs in the R-1's vernal pools that are endangered if we don't detach from the Park District. It's the R-1 homeowners that are an endangered species."

At the time, the community had only three parks — County Park on Del Playa Dr., Children's Park at Picasso and Camino del Sur roads, and an as-yet-undeveloped Anisq'Oyo Park in the center of the commercial district. One of the visions of the supporters of the Park Bond that had passed a few months earlier was to buy the larger remaining open spaces in Isla Vista, some of which had vernal pools containing several endangered species of flora and fauna.

"We have plenty of open space around us, both with the twenty or so vacant lots in the R-1 and with the University's West Campus right next door," said another R-1 property owner. "We don't need the

Park District's open space purchase plan."

Surprise Outcome

LAFCO members, in a surprise move, rejected the detachment request. Citing the small size of the Isla Vista Park District (0.55 square miles), Lompoc Mayor Eugene Stevens said that if the R-1 residents didn't use the Park District's parks, it was their own choice. Lompoc Supervisor Mutt Beattie said he thought the voters of Isla Vista were a bit "too grandiose" in their open space purchase plans, but he didn't think that detachment was the solution to what he saw as a "political" problem. Public member J. Tim Terry (Montecito) didn't think that LAFCO should get involved with how well a special district was operating: "That's up to the electorate."

So, the people in the Red Area have had to continue living with the people in the Green Area, although the battle continues into the present.

Who Was Right?

It is important to note that since 1976, the value of property in the R-1 area has increased from an average of $35,000 for a two-bedroom house to well over $700,000, while the taxes on the average R-1 property haven't much more than tripled for those homeowners who still live there. Interestingly, most of the leadership of the IVA back in 1976 are still residents there — and are still active in opposing Park District tax increases.

It is also interesting to realize that the open space that R-1 residents had at the time has almost vanished. In the 1980s, UCSB put 64 condos in the middle of the West Campus open space and have another 350 units in the planning stage. In addition, most of the remaining vacant lots in R-1 have had houses constructed on them, which began with the passage of Measure T in the 1987 water board election that provided enough water to build 250 homes in Isla Vista and Goleta.

One IVA activist verbally attacked Doug Butler at a 1988 Goleta Water Board meeting, saying that Butler was to blame for all of the open space disappearing in I.V.'s R-l neighborhood. Butler had been the leader of the campaign to pass Measure T.

But Butler shot back: "Listen, you people in the R-1 could have saved all that open space if you had supported some of the park bonds in Isla Vista. Instead, you fought against them, saving yourself $60 to $75 a year, and look what you got."

In the meantime, the Isla Vista Park District purchased some 37 acres of land in Isla Vista (some with vernal pools) over the period 1977-87, most of which would cost 10-15 times as much if they were to be purchased today. Since then, and with the assistance of the County, another 20 acres has been added to the community's inventory of parks, including the large parcel around Isla Vista Elementary School and several lots along the ocean front.

CHAPTER 10

WATER POLITICS &

THE THIRD ISLA VISTA CITYHOOD CAMPAIGN

by Carrie Topliffe

The 1980s started slowly in Isla Vista as the reality of the Reagan years set in. CETA job-training positions at community agencies were wiped out, cutting back local services dramatically. After a decade of advisory-only community government, citizen participation began to wane, as did voting in strictly local elections. This produced some dramatic results as Carrie Topliffe points out in this chapter, which originally appeared in the Isla Vista Free Press *as a two-article series in the spring of 1987. -- CL*

In November 1985, voter turnout in Isla Vista was the worst in anyone's memory, continuing a decade-long trend of declining participation by Isla Vista residents in strictly local elections. Significantly, it was the watershed year for control of the Goleta Water Board, the elected five-member body that supplies water to the then-unincorporated communities of Goleta and Isla Vista. [Goleta became a city in 2002.] After fourteen years of dominance by environmentalists, the water district fell under the control of a group of men determined to ease water restrictions for new development.

Carrie Topliffe was an elected member of the Isla Vista Park Board, 1980-84. She was also on the board of the Isla Vista Open Door Medical Clinic from 1977 through 1995. 1983 courtesy photo.

To the beleaguered citizens of Isla Vista, packed into the densest, most poorly planned community in the county, the effects would be dramatic for years to come.

What happened? What changed Isla Vista from the most dependable liberal voting bloc in the county to a seat of apathy mustering only a few thousand-vote turnout? Perhaps the answer can be found in the history of Isla Vista's place in local environmental politics.

Recall that the population of Goleta and Isla Vista together had increased from 19,000 in 1960 to 69,000 in 1970 to the point that the underlying aquifer was being over-drafted.

In 1971, Llana Sherman, Jose Martinez, and John McCord were elected to the Goleta Water Board on a platform that called for making natural resources such as water "an input into the planning process." In December of that year, they were instrumental in passing a Board-declared moratorium on all new water hook-ups, bring all new construction in Goleta and Isla Vista to a screeching halt. They justified this radical step with evidence that underground water supplies were being depleted faster than they were being replenished by natural sources. The Goleta Valley was growing larger than the environment could reliably support.

In acknowledging the connection between vital environmental resources and the human community, the Goleta Water Board was in the forefront of a nationwide move toward environmental awareness.

> *(T)he Goleta Water Board was in the forefront of a nationwide move toward environmental awareness. Growth could no longer be seen as having no limits . . . .*

A Goleta-based veterinarian, Bill Wallace moved to Isla Vista in 1970 and was elected to two terms on the Isla Vista Community Council, 1971-73. He was elected to the Goleta Water Board in 1973, then to the County board of supervisors in 1976, serving until 1996. For over 20 years, he was the widely acknowledged leader of the environmentalist movement in Santa Barbara County. This Isla Vista *Free Press* photo was taken in 1988.

Growth could no longer be seen as having no limits, nor could natural resources be stressed beyond their ability to recover without exacting a terrible future toll.

This line of thinking was echoed at UCSB, as students enrolled in Environmental Studies classes, a popular major first offered at the campus in 1970. If exposure to these ideas wasn't enough alone, Isla Vistans also had ample opportunity to experience firsthand the effects of uncontrolled growth. With its special SR (Student Residential) zoning categories, Isla Vista was created unlike any other community in the county — and was a particularly dire example of the evils of excessive growth. Isla Vista became a natural breeding ground for no-growth/stop-growth voters.

Although the 1972 voter-approved ballot initiative that validated the moratorium and established guidelines for alleviating the water shortage would have won approval without Isla Vista's vote, in future years Isla Vistans would play a crucial role in maintaining environmentalist control of the Goleta Water District's board of directors.

In fact, the election of 1973 proved to be the last time that environmentalist candidates were successful in gaining seats on the five-member Goleta Water Board without Isla Vista's votes. The election of 1973 also marked a step in Bill Wallace's ascent to power in the Goleta Valley, as the veterinarian and then-Isla Vista Community Council (IVCC) member was swept to victory to the water board. Together with slate-mate Linda Phillips, they won by a two-to-one margin. At over 42%, turnout was high throughout the District's boundaries, which stretch from Hope Ranch through Western Goleta.

(T)he election of 1973 proved to be the last time that environmentalist candidates were successful in gaining seats on the five-member Goleta Water Board without Isla Vista's votes.

Isla Vista's Role

The next water board election, in November 1975, followed a pattern that was to be replayed over and over throughout the late '70s and early '80s. Challenger Don Weaver, a UCSB professor critical of the environmentalist slate, was the top vote-getter in areas excluding Isla Vista, carrying 35 of 56 precincts. However, Isla Vista lined up solidly behind the environmentalists. When all the votes were tallied, the environmentalist slate of Sherman/Martinez/Wyner swept to victory, with an ample 822-vote margin between Wyner (who received the least votes of anyone on the slate) and fourth-place Weaver. Of 3,992 votes cast in Isla Vista, Weaver captured only 550, while Martinez and Sherman took 3,556 each (89%).

In 1977, two seats were up for election, and the pattern repeated. Environmentalists Linda Phillips and Isla Vistan Ed Maschke would have finished behind challengers Don Weaver and Steve Jones if not for Isla Vista's voters. As it was, Phillips topped the list with 7,400 votes, and Maschke nosed out Weaver with 7,016 to Weaver's 6,750 votes. Isla Vistans favored the environmentalists in margins of up to 96%, although voter turnouts in Isla Vista were beginning to decline, with only 22.6% of 12,089

Isla Vistan Ed Maschke won election to the Goleta Water Board in 1977 and was reelected in 1981. During that period, he ran the I.V. Recycling Center and started the SUNRAE solar energy project. Campaign photograph.

registered voters at the polls. In one dorm precinct where Maschke racked up 195 votes, Weaver scored six, while his slate-mate Jones tallied three. Outside of Isla Vista, only two precincts were carried by the environmentalists.

All this was enough to make some people, including UCSB Chancellor Huttenback, suggest that student residents of Isla Vista be prohibited from voting in local elections, and encouraged — or legally mandated — to vote in their parents' districts instead. Environmentalists generally shuddered at the thought of losing such a strong local, liberal constituency, and noted that local events had a profound impact on the student community, both as a group of relatively transient individuals and as a very permanent segment of the local population. As such, students were entitled to be involved as shapers of policy.

The water board elections of 1979 saw Isla Vista once again playing a crucial role in maintaining the environmentalist status quo. This time, however, environmentalist Donna Hone finished third in a three-seat race behind challengers Don Weaver and Gary McFarland, a leader in I.V.'s St. Athanasius Church (see Chapter 12). For the first time in eight years, the environmentalist slate was not entirely victorious. Hone joined

The . . . election in 1981 saw incumbent environmentalists Ed Maschke and Pat Shewczyk winning the hotly contested election thanks to an 85% margin of victory in I.V. Without Isla Vista's votes, challenger Larry Lane would have placed first over Maschke, with Shewczyk finishing fourth behind challenger Henry Schulte.

1977 victors Maschke and Phillips to maintain an environmentalist majority on the board, but with her victory came the chilling realization of how close the environmentalists were to losing control.

The events of 1983 marked the beginning of the end for environmentalist control of the Goleta Water Board, according to Ed Maschke, who lost his seat — and with it, the Board majority — in 1985.

The next election, in 1981, saw incumbent environmentalist Ed Maschke and Pat Shewczyk winning the hotly contested election thanks to an 85% margin of victory in I.V. Without Isla Vista's votes, challenger Larry Lane would have placed first over Maschke, with Shewczyk finishing fourth behind challenger Henry Schulte.

The Beginning of the End

The events of 1983 marked the beginning of the end for environmentalist control of the Goleta Water Board, according to Ed Maschke, who lost his seat — and with it, the Board majority — in 1985. By 1983, things had changed. Environmentalists had been in control of the Goleta Water Board for almost ten years, and the pendulum of political change was swinging.

For one thing, the moratorium was springing leaks, as developers with large projects found it cost-effective to sink wells to provide the water they needed, thus circumventing the moratorium's restrictions. Large-scale industrial and commercial projects were breaking ground right and left, and fruit orchards were falling to housing developments.

Not the least of the problems faced by the environmentalists was the simple fact of their success. As with any group holding power for close to a decade, the environmentalists discovered that with a track record comes criticism. It's one thing to be a challenger, full of wild promises and quixotic goals, and quite another to spend years making difficult decisions, each one bound to alienate at least someone. A groundswell of blame was being placed on the environmentalists for everything from high housing prices to foul-tasting water.

Meanwhile, Isla Vistans were developing an agenda of their own. Although water board campaign rhetoric always focused on the polarity between developers and environmentalists, land-use planning questions remained somewhat outside the scope of campaign debate, as the water board could do little other than issue blanket denials of new water hookups. With planning decisions still in the hands of the County board of supervisors, citizens of the Goleta Valley felt they could expect little from the County but the type of haphazard, poorly planned growth that was characteristic of Isla Vista.

The election of 1983 found Isla Vista fielding its own environmentalist candidate as dissention developed over the long-range options for growth control in the Goleta Valley. I had a front row seat for the events of that election, because I was the Isla Vista environmentalist candidate.

An Isla Vista Agenda

Isla Vistans had been pushing for separate cityhood for a number of years. Proposals to hold an election on I.V. on becoming a city had been rejected by the Local Agency Formation Commission (LAFCO) in 1973 and 1976 (see Chapter 5). But in 1983, another attempt was gathering steam as the result of an IVCC advisory election in November 1982 that found 2-1 support for independent cityhood over joining a combined city with Goleta.

With its unique demographics and dense, urbanized population, Isla Vista seemed a natural for cityhood. Ironically, this became a

John Buttny in 1988. In 1982, Buttny and County Supervisor Bill Wallace ran a slate of candidates for the Isla Vista Community Council that supported a combined city of Isla Vista and Goleta. However, a slate supporting an independent City of Isla Vista won all seats. When Wallace and his Goleta allies chose Buttny to run on a slate of three candidates for the Goleta Water Board in 1983, it provoked a rebellion in Isla Vista that resulted in the fielding of an "independent Environmentalist" -- Carrie Topliffe. In 2004, Buttny ran for what had been Wallace's seat on the board of supervisors on a pro-I.V. Cityhood platform. Isla Vista *Free Press* photo.

point of contention between many Isla Vistans and their environmentalist allies in Goleta. These Goletans were afraid to be isolated in a separate city, where environmental concerns might lose out without the voting support of Isla Vista.

As the Isla Vista Community Council mounted another incorporation attempt in 1983, the issue came to a head as it was rumored that John Buttny, IVCC executive director, who was under fire from a majority of his board of directors for his competing efforts a joint I.V./Goleta cityhood proposal, was to be the "Isla Vista" candidate on the environmentalist's slate with Donna Hone (up for re-election with three seats vacant) for the water board. More than one Isla Vistan felt that after courting Isla Vista's support through so many years of water board campaigns, the Goletans should be more supportive of Isla Vista's long-cherished desire for self-government. Buttny was seen as a candidate many Isla Vistans could not support.

> *Resentment grew in some Isla Vista circles because of the unwillingness of the leadership of the Goleta environmentalists to share power with Isla Vista in the selection of candidates for an office that required such significant Isla Vista voter support.*

In 1983, Carrie Topliffe ran for the Goleta Water Board as an "Independent Environmentalist" after negotiations failed to include her on a three-member slate chosen by the leadership of the Goleta environmentalists. Instead, the Goleta folks initially chose an opponent of I.V. Cityhood, John Buttny, as the "Isla Vista" member of their slate, but later dropped him. Although she won every I.V./UCSB precinct handily, she did so poorly in Goleta that she wound up placing sixth overall. Campaign button designed by Jim Crandall.

That's where I came in. An eight-year resident of Isla Vista, I had been successfully elected to the Isla Vista Park Board in 1980, and had many contacts in town from my numerous civic involvements.

I was urged by several Isla Vista friends to run as a balance to Buttny on the environmentalist slate. But when I approached Donna Hone, she said that all three positions were filled on the environmentalist's slate.

Resentment grew in some Isla Vista circles because of the unwillingness of the leadership of the Goleta environmentalists to share power with Isla Vista in the selection of candidates for an office that required such significant Isla Vista voter support. There were some weeks of discussion between us, but no compromise was reached.

I ended up running as an "independent" environmentalist.

The irony was that Buttny was later

The irony was that Buttny was later pressured by the Goleta-based environmentalists to withdraw from the race . . . when information surfaced about his felony arrest during the 1960's antiwar movement.

pressured by the Goleta-based environmentalists to withdraw from the race (although his name remained on the ballot) when information surfaced about his felony arrest during the 1960's antiwar movement.

At the time, Glen Lazof, a member of the winning slate to the IVCC in 1982, said of Buttny and the Goleta people: "They picked him for the wrong reasons, they kept him for the wrong reasons, and they dumped him for the wrong reasons!"

These events and stresses made it a difficult campaign, and the results were upsetting. Hone managed to keep her seat, finishing third to fellow incumbents Don Weaver and Gary MacFarland. Although I gathered 67% of the vote in the I.V./UCSB area and came in first in every I.V./UCSB precinct, my support in Goleta was very weak and I finished a disappointing sixth overall for the

Continued on p. 105

The Third Isla Vista Cityhood Campaign (1983-84)

The November 1982 Isla Vista Community Council (IVCC) election of representatives and plebiscite on local government options was one of the most pivotal in the community's history.

Over 3,000 people voted in the election, a much larger turnout than anyone familiar with Isla Vista at that time thought possible. Most surprisingly, the

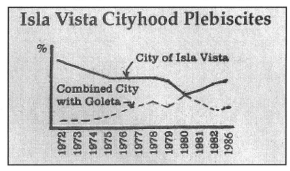

Isla Vista *Free Press* graphic.

entire slate of candidates supporting a combined city with Goleta was defeated by candidates supporting an independent City of Isla Vista.

Then-IVCC Executive Director John Buttny and County Supervisor Bill Wallace were the leaders of the strong campaign for the slate supporting a combined city with Goleta. Buttny resigned shortly after the election, taking a similar position with the Rochdale Housing Co-op. He later became Wallace's top aide.

Several people who went on to become important leaders in Isla Vista were elected to the IVCC in that momentous election. Glen Lazof and Marc Borgman were the leaders of the pro-Isla Vista Cityhood campaign. Lazof later became the general manager of the Isla Vista Recreation & Park District and Borgman worked for the Park District for

Continued on p. 104

1983-84 Cityhood *continued from p. 103*

several years. Mike Boyd was also elected to the IVCC in 1982 and later to the Park Board. In 1988, he ran unsuccessfully against Wallace for County supervisor. Mitch Stockton and Diane Conn, who would later win seats on the Park Board, also were on the winning slate in the 1982 IVCC election. Conn is a member of the current Park Board (2008).

There's no question that the 1982 IVCC election inspired both Carrie Topliffe's 1983 candidacy as an "independent Environmentalist" for the Goleta Water Board and the third Isla Vista Cityhood campaign.

The 1982-83 IVCC quickly set about preparing a new incorporation proposal to submit to LAFCO. The completed proposal was accompanied by a petition containing the signatures of 25% of Isla Vista's registered voters, although only a 5%-petition was required.

LAFCO demanded an Environmental Impact Report on the proposal as a way to study the finances of the proposed city. County supervisors required that IVCC pay $3,400 of the $13,400 cost of the EIR. The money was quickly collected in a series of fundraisers and solicitations.

1984 Isla Vista Incorporation Proposal cover graphic by Jim Crandall featuring the I.V. Tree.

The results of the EIR indicated that, with an $18-per-year per-resident tax increase, a City of Isla Vista could roughly triple the current level of municipal-type services supplied by the County, and still have over $10 million in the bank at the end of its first decade.

The UCSB Administration again opposed the plan, announcing their opposition several months before they put up $26,000 for a San Francisco consultant to do a hatchet job on the proposal. The UC Regents supported the local Administration, except for the Student Regent who followed the UCSB Associated Students' endorsement of an independent City of Isla Vista.

LAFCO turned down the proposal 4-1, with County Supervisor Bill Wallace, a former resident of Isla Vista and an elected member of the 1972-73 IVCC that submitted the first Incorporation Proposal in 1973, the only supportive vote. However, Wallace mounted no serious effort to gain the support of other LAFCO members, at least two of who were his allies on countywide environmental issues.   *-- CL*

Water Politics *continued from p. 103*

for the three contested seats.

The next year held a big surprise, as the environmentalists were forced to undergo another election challenge a year ahead of schedule. In 1984, led by developer Jerry Beaver, a recall campaign was mounted against the water board majority. Although Ed Maschke, Pat Shewczyk and Donna Hone were successful in holding on to their seats, the campaign was taxing financially and emotionally.

Traditionally, a turnout of three to four thousand in Isla Vista was expected up to that point. However, in 1985 only 2,082 actually voted, or 14.9% of the registered voters, and of those, only 62% voted for the environmentalist slate. The loss of Maschke and Shewczyk's seats could be attributed directly to the erosion of the Isla Vista bloc vote.

"We had to go through four elections in two years," laments Maschke in explaining that this period was very difficult on the Goleta environmentalists that were active in the 1981 and 1983 water board campaigns, in Bill Wallace's third district supervisorial re-election campaign in 1984, and then in the 1985 Water Board election. "It was a tremendous drain on our financial resources, as well as physically draining on everybody."

The results were critical. After ten years of dominance, the environmentalists lost control of the Goleta Water Board in 1985.

"People just generally took the threat of us losing both our seats not nearly as seriously as they had in the past," says Maschke, attributing this to the overwhelming support the environmentalists received in the recall election of 1984.

Maschke also speculated that the 1985 election was the one in which the difference between the environmentalists and their opponents was most blurred in the minds of the voters.

"The developers always posture themselves as having the same positions as us," Maschke says. "The only difference (they say) is that they could do a better job. In the last election, they were just successful in hiding the source of their money."

Ultimately, however, it was probably Isla Vista that dealt the lethal blow.

For some years, it was obvious that students were becoming more conservative, more interested in finances than social issues. As one indicator, the popularity of campus majors was changing. In 1975, there were 664 undergraduates in the Economics Department; by 1985, there were 2,281. In comparison, the Environmental Studies Program, first offered as a major in 1970, saw a steady decrease in enrollment by 1985.

Cathy Buchanan, an Environmental Studies graduate who worked on the Maschke/Schewzyk campaign in 1981, noted the change in student values since her first undergraduate days in 1977.

"In those years, the environmental movement was still new and big, there was a greater awareness of the interrelatedness of natural systems than there is now," she said. "Nowadays, students don't seem to put an economic value on natural resources. Actually, environmental resources, because of their interrelatedness, have a very high economic value, because when you destroy one thing you're actually destroying everything."

As students became more conservative, they were also began mouthing a traditional piece of conservative thought. Voter registration workers reported that students were often choosing to disenfranchise themselves, claiming that as transient residents of the area, it was not proper that they vote here.

"Historically, those arguments have been used by the people who didn't want students to have the vote. But to hear students adopt those attitudes just blew me out. I was amazed," said Ed Maschke. "This line of thought did not acknowledge that students, as a constituency, have a very permanent and significant profile in the local community."

In Isla Vista, the result was a dismal combination of poor turnout and lessened support for the environmentalists. Traditionally, a turnout of three to four thousand in Isla Vista was expected up to that point. However, in 1985 only 2,082 actually voted, or 14.9% of the registered voters, and of those, only 62% voted for the environmentalist slate. The loss of Maschke and Shewczyk's seats could be attributed directly to the erosion of the Isla Vista bloc vote. An additional 1,310 voters casting ballots for the environmentalist slate would have nudged them to victory.

Instead, Chuck Bennett and Jim Thompson swept to victory, to join incumbents Don Weaver and Gary MacFarland in a new majority pledging to "get out of the land-use planning business."

In other words, they were going to issue water permits to new construction projects whether they had water or not.

Note: The conservative control of the water board reignited a building boom in Goleta that didn't subside until Goleta became a city in 2002 and only let up in Isla Vista when the developers ran out of vacant lots.

However, the Isla Vista Master Plan, approved by the County board of supervisors in 2007, allows for increased densities and up to 1,450 more dwelling units. And UCSB's Long Range Development Plan currently under review calls for upping the 2007 fall enrollment of 21,410 to 25,000 by the year 2025. -- C.L.

Today Carrie Topliffe is a division head at the County of Santa Barbara. Courtesy photo.

Vote Turnout In the Isla Vista/UCSB Precincts

The trends noted in this chapter continued in 1987 and 1989.

In the 1987 election, with a combined city of Isla Vista & Goleta also on the ballot, only 1,500 people turned out to vote in the Isla Vista/UCSB precincts. The combined city was rejected 54%-46% in the Isla Vista/UCSB precincts and by a greater margin in Goleta. In 1989, only 750 voted -- just 6.2% of those registered.

However, in both cases I.V.'s support of the environmentalists was crucial to returning them to control of the Goleta Water Board. That is, in both elections environmentalists lost in Goleta but won by large enough margins in Isla Vista to give them a majority of seats on the board of directors.

After the 1987 election, the Isla Vista *Free Press* conducted a survey of 100 Isla Vista residents. Seventy-five percent of those interviewed said they would have turned out to vote if the selection Isla Vista's police chief and/or rent control had been on the ballot. Such options could have been on the ballot if Isla Vista had been a city at the time.

Low voter turnout seems to be evident only in local elections. In the 1988 presidential election, for example, almost 9,000 people voted in the I.V./UCSB precincts. And while Isla Vista had dropped off to being only 65% registered Democrats, the Democratic congressional candidate took 89% of the votes against the entrenched Republican, who won re-election in a very close race.

This pattern has persisted in recent years when 9,059 Isla Vista and UCSB residents voted in the 2000 presidential election and 9,667 in 2004 -- probably the record for voter turnout in the I.V./UCSB precincts. However, only 4,761 voted in the 2002 governor's race and 4,547 in 2006.

In the June 2008 primary for County supervisor, only 1,961 people turned out in Isla Vista and on campus. According to the Sept. 18, 2008 UCSB *Daily Nexus*, this was "the lowest turnout in 28 years, with roughly half as many people voting this year than four years earlier."

It should be pointed out that in that election four years earlier, John Buttny was a candidate for County supervisor running on a platform supporting Isla Vista Cityhood. While he lost overall to Brook Firestone, he won I.V./UCSB handily. No candidates supported I.V. Cityhood in the 2008 primary.

Finally, while the County Elections Office indicates that there are over 12,500 registered voters in Isla Vista/UCSB precincts in almost all years, there probably are only about 10,000 live bodies. The rest have probably moved on but have not yet been purged from the rolls.

-- CL

CHAPTER 11

THE I.V. CLINIC BUILDING'S INTRIGUING STORY

Convicted murderer Jack Quaglino was paroled in 1989. And the Isla Vista Medical Clinic expanded its building, known since 1970 as the Isla Vista Community Service Center, in 1990.

Why are these two events mentioned together? It's all part of Isla Vista's dark past. Murder, intrigue, sex scandals, and more, figure in the history of the building — one of the most valuable assets ever owned by an Isla Vista community agency until it was gobbled up in a merger with two Santa Barbara neighborhood clinics in the late 1990s.

The Isla Vista Community Services Center with the pond in Anisq'Oyo Park in the foreground. 1988 photo from the Isla Vista *Free Press*.

The Old Days

Two of the buildings thrown up in Isla Vista during the development orgy of the 1960s was a 4,500-square-foot office complex consisting of a one-story building at 966 Embarcadero del Mar and a two-story one behind at 970. The local pharmacist, Phil Quaglino, financed the complex, but it never really caught on. Even before the Bank of America was burned, which left in its wake a 10% decrease in UCSB enrollment and a 25% vacancy rate in I.V. apartments, the complex was never fully occupied.

Between 1970 and 1976, the Isla Vista Community Service Center Corporation held the back building under a master lease. The IVCSC housed several community agencies, most of which paid their rent through grants from the county, the UC Regents, and even the Bank of America. Tribute money to prevent any further civil unrest, some people called these funds.

It was during this period that "Pete the Freak" painted a mural on the north end of the building, dubbing it the "Isla Vista People's Center." That mural, along with one of a joint-smoking freak on the south end of the building, were both painted over during the remodeling of the building in 1989-90.

During the early 1970s, Suite C in the front building housed the Isla Vista Community Council (IVCC) and its Planning Commission (where a Mexican restaurant, The Cantina, is now), and Suite D held the local, weekly newspaper, the *Town Crier* (where an Asian Indian restaurant exists today). Also at the time, an organic grocery store (Sun and Earth) held forth where the Deja Vu bar and grill is today, while the Rosarito restaurant dishes up Mexican food in Suite A, the former home of a dry cleaning establishment.

Besides the Isla Vista Medical Clinic, the IVCSC held the first community credit union in the country, a legal collective, Switchboard (a 24-hour hotline for people in distress), and a counseling service.

Pete the Freak painted this mural on the north side of the Isla Vista Community Services Building in 1971, noting all the agencies then housed in the building. The mural was painted over when the Isla Vista Medical Clinic remodeled the building in 1989. 1988 photo from the Isla Vista *Free Press*.

By the mid-1970s, the Isla Vista Recreation and Park District had been established, and with its financial power forced its parent organization — the IVCC — into a smaller office in the back building (you know how rebellious youth can be).

By then too, the Orgo grocery store had gone out-of-business, as had the community newspaper (the latter's space first having been taken over by a blood-collecting business).

Up For Sale

Having reached retirement age shortly after 1970, Quaglino sold his pharmacy (now the Hempwise head shop) and placed his office complex on the market. For several years it was available for $139,500. The IVCC tried desperately to find the finances to purchase the complex to make permanent its status as a community service center. Ross Pumphrey, the administrator of the IVCSC corporation in the early 1970s, and Lauri Bacon, IVCC's planning director 1974-75, together submitted at least twenty grant proposals to secure the building, all to no avail.

> *(I)f Isla Vista had formed a city in 1973 or 1975, the community could have easily purchased the buildings and made them City Hall.*

Even the University refused to help out, even though the UC Regents report after the 1970 riots (See Chapter 3: The Trow Report and Appendix A) had strongly recommended that UCSB start holding classes in Isla Vista and put many of its community-relations personnel there.

> [The UCSB Administration should] work with community members in constructing new community institutions . . . protecting Isla Vista ventures in their efforts to become community institutions . . . , to make UCSB services to students available where they live (i.e., in Isla Vista), . . . continue UCSB's active role in the development of the Isla Vista Community Center . . . (and) develop similar student-oriented services as new or different community needs become clear.
>
> THE TROW REPORT, page 87

During the late-1970s, while IVCC was attempting to secure funding to purchase both buildings for the bargain price of $140,000, the UCSB Administration twice declined a request to contribute $50,000 to the project.

It got worse: The recommendation from a student committee to allocate $50,000 from a student registration fee surplus, which at the time was over $4 million, to purchase the Isla Vista Service Center buildings was vetoed by then-Chancellor Robert Huttenback.

And then-State Assemblyman Gary K. Hart was unable to find any state resources to purchase the building.

Of course, if Isla Vista had formed a city in 1973 or 1975, the community could have easily purchased the buildings and made them City Hall.

Breakthrough!

However, in 1976, while I was working in a CETA slot as the Economic Development Coordinator for the IVCC, I caught the County trying to hold the second required public hearing for a $3-million pot of federal community development money on the same day as the first hearing.

A quick reading of the federal regulations told me this wasn't the correct procedure. So between the morning and afternoon hearings, I chased down the staff person responsible and threatened to blow his cover if some of the money didn't come to Isla Vista.

We found in the regs that a "neighborhood center" qualified for the grant, which was close enough to a "community services center" for me. The staffer and I quickly reached a figure of $50,000 as appropriate for the project, which was then approved by the supervisors on a 5-0 vote. Of course, the Supes had no idea how this project had been added to the staff's recommendations between the two hearings.

With such a large down payment, I figured the community would easily be able to find a bank — or even Quaglino himself — to finance the balance of the selling price.

We took our situation to Quaglino and he agreed to sell us the two buildings based on the County's down payment, although somewhat reluctantly because he didn't like it that it might take up to six months for the County to actually release the funds to him.

Celebration Turns Sour

We were so excited, we held a party that lasted well into the next day! Local newspapers heralded the accomplishment that Isla Vistans had made another major step in our struggle for political and economic self-determination.

Isla Vista Community Council Representative Lisa Pompa and IVCC staffer Carmen Lodise hanging the "Town Hall" sign on the IVCC's office at 966 Embarcadero del Mar. Photograph from the *IVCC Newsletter*, March 1977.

The excitement didn't last long, however. About 10:30 the next night a Dr. Ken Frank called me at home, telling me he was the new owner of the Isla Vista Service Center and the front building. I thought he was a crank caller, so I hung up. But Frank called back immediately and assured me he had just settled a deal with Quaglino to purchase both buildings.

As if he was trying to be a nice guy, Frank told me he was willing to sell the community the back building for $100,000. Since he was buying both buildings for $140,000 and both had equal floor space, I immediately saw that this was not a good deal.

The next day I called Quaglino and he confirmed Frank's story. He explained that his son Jack was about to go on trial for murdering his wife by running her over with a car while she was jogging on Cathedral Oaks Road in Goleta. The old man needed $25,000 immediately to pay for a hotshot attorney to defend his son. He simply decided he couldn't wait for the money from the County and had accepted Frank's offer.

Incidentally, this was the second time one of the younger Quaglino's wives died under weird circumstances.

The great irony was that Frank had found out about the buildings being for sale by reading newspaper accounts of the IVCC grant from the County. He had apparently read something separately about Quaglino's financial problems.

It turned out that Dr. Frank was one of several partners in the blood-collecting business in the front building. The company was called Plasma Quest and they paid virile college students in need of spending money $6-a-pint for their blood.

How the Clinic Acquired the I.V. Service Center

Frank made good on his offer to sell the community the back building, even assisting in the drawing up of a very creative financing plan.

But the situation became more complex before it cleared up. Two of the conditions of the federal grant were that

The Isla Vista Medical Clinic can be seen in the background from People's Park on Embarcadero del Norte. That's Perfect Park off to the left.

the neighborhood center had to be owned by a non-profit agency and that agency couldn't be a unit of local government. The IVCC was a for-profit corporation, so it could take stands on political issues, and, in its capacity as the community's official advisory body to county government (a 'municipal advisory council'), was a unit of the county. Thus, IVCC/MAC wasn't eligible to own the building, even though one of its employees had scored the grant.

It was decided rather quickly to give the building to the Isla Vista Open Door Medical Clinic, the oldest and most stable tenant in the building. The clinic had recently transformed from Dr. Dave Bearman's private practice into the non-profit Isla Vista Health Projects, Inc. (IVHP).

No formal agreement was made between the IVCC and the clinic. However, the discussion at the time made it clear that the building was to belong to 'the community,' but that the clinic was to be the legal owner because of the restrictions of the grant.

My hope was that the equity in the building could eventually be used as part of a larger effort to buy up

I.V. apartments, converting them to co-ops.

But the clinic has always used the building as its own asset, although IVHP has kept the rents to its

tenants to about one-half the market rate. These tenants have been I.V. non-profit agencies for the most part, although UCSB and the County have established liaison offices there in the 1990s. On average, only two or three of the clinic's board of directors were I.V. residents at any one time, although several others were likely to have lived in Isla Vista in previous years. To my knowledge, no current or former Isla Vista residents have been on the board of directors of the Santa Barbara Neighborhood Clinics, the non-profit corporation that absorbed the Isla Vista Medical Clinic in the late 1990s.

Today, the clinic is widely respected as a low-cost, quality medical care facility. It receives nearly 6,000 patient visits a year, about one-half of who have traditionally come from beyond Isla Vista.

Then-State Assemblyman Jack O'Connell (left), then-County Supervisor Bill Wallace (center), and then-State Senator Gary K. Hart turn over the first shovel of dirt to begin the construction project to remodel the Isla Vista Medical Building, March 22, 1989. Clinic ED Carole Edson is presiding from the podium. O'Connell is currently the State Superintendent of Schools. Photograph by Caroline White for the Isla Vista *Free Press*.

Life Goes On

Some years later Ken Frank later sold the front building of the complex he bought from Phil Quaglino for a reported $395,000 — not a bad profit. At about the same time, Santa Barbara's Cottage Hospital revoked his permit to practice there after he was accused of sexually molesting one of his patients. He went on to establish one of the 24-hour, private medical clinics that sprang up in the 1980s throughout in the area, and for months his voice could be heard on the radio several times a day hawking his services. However, his clinic was eventually absorbed by Samsun Clinic.

Jack Quaglino was convicted of the murder charge and spent twelve years in jail. He was paroled in Ventura in 1989.

Life goes on in I.V., but some of its stories still raise eyebrows.

Note: **See the Addendum to Chapter 12** on page 127 for recent changes at the Isla Vista Medical Clinic.

CHAPTER 12

THE ST. ATHANASIUS CHURCH AND SAVING PERFECT PARK

By the end of the 1980s, Isla Vista's St. Athanasius Church had become the most powerful economic and political force in the community.

From its humble beginnings in the early 1970s as the UCSB chapter of the right-wing Campus Crusade for Christ, the influence of the church had grown to the point that their membership had collectively become one of the biggest property owners in Isla Vista, its spokesmen routinely offered up input in community governance in defense of the Church's interests, and its members held important elected positions in Goleta Valley politics.

At the time, slow-growth County Supervisor Bill Wallace, a former Isla Vista resident, said, "Individually, they're all really nice people, but politically, they certainly are pro-growth."

Mike Boyd, a member of the I.V. Park Board and a candidate for the

The St. Athanasius Church building at 976 Embarcadero del Mar, which was purchased in 1984. Perfect Park is off to the right and the Isla Vista Medical Clinic building can be seen in the right background. I.V. *Free Press* photo.

Goleta Water Board in 1987 against two of the church's members, Gary McFarland and David Lewis, called them "I.V.'s moonies" and a "cult" during the campaign. The reaction of one church leader, John Sommers, was to call Boyd a "fascist."

Other people have called them "I.V.'s moral majority" — a description not meant to be a compliment.

While the relationship between the church and Isla Vista's elected community leadership could best be described as strained, it wasn't until the church announced plans to build a 19,000-square-foot temple in Perfect Park, that a full-scale war broke out.

The EOC

"St. Athanasius" is the third name of this congregation since the leadership began moving to Isla Vista in the late 1960s. Until 1979, they were the Grace Catholic Church. From 1979 until early 1989, they were the Evangelical Orthodox Church, or EOC. But, in the late 1980s they became the St. Athanasius Church when they affiliated with the 200,000,000-member Eastern Orthodox Church worldwide.

EOC will be used throughout this chapter.

The announced purpose of the early church members was to subdue the libertine impulses rampant among Isla Vista's youth. A large mural that used to grace the south side of their church building at 976 Embarcadero del Mar (across from the Bagel Cafe) depicted a lion being subdued by a lamb. Most people interpreted this to mean the church (the lamb) will subdue the community (the lion) though its gentle ways.

Only some of their ways, however, can be called gentle.

Community Impacts

The impact of the EOC on Isla Vista community governance has been immense. For example, members of the church maintained two parks in Isla Vista for several years — parks belonging to the Isla Vista Recreation and Park District. These properties were not being maintained adequately in their opinion, so they decided to show the Park District what could be done with some real volunteer effort.

There was no question that the parks, one in the 6600 block of Sueño Road and the other in the 6600 block of Pasado/Trigo Roads, did look much better because of their efforts. The Park District resumed responsibility for their maintenance after I.V. voters approved a tax increase in 1988.

In addition, volunteers from the EOC are the distributors of hundreds of pounds of free surplus government food to I.V.'s needy families each month.

They also have been steady participants in Isla Vista community politics, with at least one member attending most I.V. Park Board and

Trigo/Pasado Park in 2008. For a year-or-so in the mid-1980s, EOC volunteers maintained this park before the Park District had water to grow and maintain grass. The Park District reassumed responsibility for it and all other District-owned properties following a voter-approved tax increase in 1984. Measure T water arrived in 1988.

Isla Vista Federation meetings. The Federation was a collection of representatives of Isla Vista interest groups appointed by the County supervisor, which came into existence in the late 1980s and pretty much forced the Isla Vista Community Council to disband in 1987. It was disbanded in 2002 by then County Supervisor Gail Marshall due to lack of attendance at its monthly meetings.

In fact, the EOC had its own seat in the Federation, making its political presence equivalent to the local homeowners association, the business association, and such elected bodies as the I.V. Park Board and the UCSB Associated Students' Legislative Council.

. . . the EOC had its own seat in the Federation, making its political presence equivalent to the local homeowners association, the business association, and such elected bodies as the I.V. Park Board and the UCSB Associated Students' Legislative Council.

It should be noted that the church did not represent all churches in the Federation — it represented itself.

It should be noted that the church did not represent all churches in the Federation — it represented itself.

EOC members have run for several positions of leadership in the community — both in Isla Vista and Goleta. The example of McFarland and Lewis on the Goleta Water Board (McFarland elected, Lewis appointed) has been mentioned previously. But, Lewis is also an elected member of the I.V. Sanitary Board where he was able in 1987 to get a fellow church member (Harvey Gish) appointed to a 2-1/2 year term resulting from a vacancy Lewis helped arrange. In 1980, a slate of three church members ran for the Isla Vista Park Board hoping to gain a majority on the board, which has a total of five members. However, all three were defeated handily. In 1986, another slate of three tried again. This time all three were disqualified by the County Elections Office, either for incomplete petitions or because they did not live within the I.V. Park District boundaries. And in 1988, one church member ran for the Isla Vista Park Board on a slate with I.V. homeowners, but lost.

Church Origins

Most of the leadership of the church moved to Isla Vista in the late 1960s and early 1970s. In a series the UCSB *Daily Nexus* ran on the church in 1979, one church leader is quoted as saying: "Our Lord Jesus Christ told us to come to Isla Vista and to get involved."

According to the *Daily Nexus* series, "the church draws its funds from a 10-percent tithe (and)... the tithe is actually paid by all members." The series also quotes church member John Sommers saying that there were about 150 families in the EOC, a total of about 375 members, who live in Isla Vista and Goleta. However, during the 1989 County hearings on their proposed new building, the church said it consisted of only 64 families, 48 of which live in Isla Vista, and about 250 total members. It would seem that to the newspaper, they were trying to puff themselves up; to the County they were trying to slide under the radar.

Most EOC families are homeowners, but not all. Many own income property in I.V. Almost all are involved with the Isla Vista Association, a middle-class homeowners group that is much alienated from the majority community.

The philosophy of the church is strongly flavored by the Eastern Orthodox Church, but with some influences from Martin Luther and other reformers. "Basically, they are fundamentalists," the *Daily Nexus* series stated.

It is widely held that leadership within the church is male-dominated, with women having no say in establishing church policy. However, this could not be confirmed.

It was in the late 1970s that Church members began to run for community offices. One member is quoted in the UCSB *Daily Nexus* saying that, "We feel that the Holy Spirit spoke to several of us" about getting involved in community politics.

> *It was in the late 1970s that Church members began to run for community offices. One member is quoted in the UCSB* Daily Nexus *saying that, "We feel that the Holy Spirit spoke to several of us" about getting involved in community politics.*

Political Impacts

While their results have been mixed in this effort, the EOC's positions have been critical to the outcome of the several important community issues on which they have chosen to take a stand.

For example:

■ 10 out of 13 of the speakers at the County board of supervisors hearing who opposed the establishment of a campsite in the 6700 block of Sueño Road, which would have saved Tipi Village (see Chapter 7), were members of the church (UCSB *Daily Nexus*, 10/18/79, page 1). The campsite re-zoning was rejected by County supervisors.

■ Most of the speakers against Isla Vista residents having an election on becoming an independent "city" during the 1985 LAFCO hearings were EOC members, although they didn't identify themselves as such.

■ Many of the speakers in 1987 who spoke during the public hearing in favor of the County establishing a ban on open containers of alcohol were members of the EOC, although they again did not identify themselves as such. Most of their comments related to the horrors of the 1986 Halloween event that had drawn some 25-30,000 people — a total surprise to everyone. They asked the Supes to "give us permanent residents protection from the transient students."

The sight of so many middle-class families at public hearings impresses policy-makers beyond Isla Vista. These are people that the policy-makers can identify with, not the "transient" students. This has always been a major problem with getting community-supported policies implemented in a town that the median length of residency has been estimated to be 26 months, despite this being not much different from the statewide median of 32 months.

The church also established its stature with the UCSB Administration. In 1989, when UCSB set up a hiring committee to interview for a new liaison position in Isla Vista, the person representing the "community" was one of the deacons in the church, according to Mike Stowers, the then-A.S. President, who also served on the committee.

The Original Temple

The EOC purchased their current church building at 976 Embarcadero del Mar about 1980. In 1977, the I.V. Park District had attempted to purchase the site in order to establish a community center, but gave up because of the high asking price. And we lived to be sorry for our timidity.

Actually, this was all my fault and I count it as the biggest mistake I made in my four years on the Park Board, 1976-80. We should have bought the EOC building right then and there. But it was early on in spending the $1.15 million bond money approved by Isla Vista voters in 1975 and our assessor said the building and property was worth only $90,000, whereas the owners (Jerkowitz & Saunders) started out asking for $145,000 and were holding out for $129,000. The Park Board majority didn't want to set a precedent that we'd pay so much more than our assessor's value because then a lot of owners of other parcels might hold out for more money, too.

Over several weeks of negotiations, the Park Board majority went as high as $115,000 as I recall, but then J&S announced they had

Little Acorn Park on Embarcadero del Mar at El Embarcadero. It lies across the street from the EOC building (white object, middle-left of picture) and Perfect Park, which stretches off to the right in this Isla Vista *Free Press* photo. The Isla Vista Medical Clinic building can be seen beyond Perfect Park (middle-right) as can the windmill in Anisq'Oyo in the distance (center). The re-built lath-house (left) of the former nursery was removed in mid-2008. The property was purchased in the 1977 by the I.V. Park District after the board of directors gave up trying to buy the EOC's building.

signed a 7-year lease with the EOC that the I.V. Park District would have to honor if we bought the building at ANY price.

Being impatient young people, we gave up the battle for the EOC building at that point and bought the Little Acorn Nursery property across the street for $165,000, with the intent to build Isla Vista's community center there. The larger Little Acorn property had a water meter and could be built on, a major positive during the 15-year moratorium on new water hook-ups (see Chapter 10).

Soon, however, plans to establish a community center on the Little Acorn property were put on hold indefinitely when a 1980 advisory election indicated 54%-46% that voters would prefer that a community center be established without constructing a new building.

It was only a few years later that I realized that the EOC building was the original Bank of America

site Even 40 years later, "BANK" painted on the sidewalk at the front of three parking spaces can still be seen. If I had known that at the time, I would have paid the $129,000 and Isla Vista would have had a community center all these years — and without building on open space.

Today Isla Vista remains the only town in the county without a community center.

The EOC Buys Perfect Park

In 1984, the church purchased the large vacant property at the top of the Embarcadero loop adjacent to their church building.

Widely known as Perfect Park, this property was the site of hundreds of concerts and community events during the late 1960s and early 1970s. It was also the site of arrests and beatings by police on June 10, 1970, near the end of the civil disturbances of that period (see Chapter 2). Because of its historical significance, the Park District also attempted to purchase this property in the late 1970s, but the owners turned down an offer in the neighborhood of $350,000. In

Three parking spaces on the north side of the EOC building still indicate some 40 years later that the building was the original Bank of American branch in Isla Vista.

rejecting the offer, the owner, a physician from Santa Monica, said that he didn't want to sell his property to "the community" because Isla Vistans kept voting to continue the water hook-up moratorium, which had prevented him from developing his property. There was some mention of his desire to put a Safeway Grocery store on the property.

A church member, John Sommers, told a reporter for the Isla Vista *Free Press* in 1987 that the church had paid considerably less than $350,000 for the property and if they could get a water permit, they would like to build a new temple at the Perfect Park site. Further, he said they would like to construct "a two-story building that we could sell off as an office site if we had to."

When this comment was introduced during County Planning Commission hearings on their building plans, church leaders never challenged the veracity of the report, insisting only that Sommers had not been authorized to make such a statement.

New EOC Temple?

In November 1987, the voters of Isla Vista and Goleta approved Measure T, an amendment to the moratorium on new hook-ups that had existed since 1972. Measure T set aside enough water to build 250 homes, some water for park irrigation and some for non-profit organizations to build such as churches. With two of its members sitting on the Goleta Water Board, the EOC got its water permit.

In addition, the church then asked and received from the Goleta Water Board a 10-year limitation on the building having to be a church, fueling speculation that they did indeed have plans to sell off their new building sometime in the future.

In early 1988, the EOC threw down the gauntlet to those who considered Perfect Park a significant relic of Isla Vista's history by submitting plans to the County for a new two-story, 19,000-square-foot

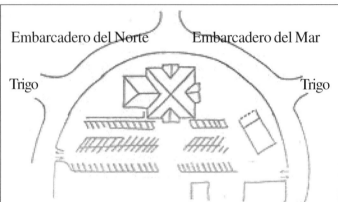

A schematic drawing of the "temple" and parking lot the EOC proposed to build on their vacant lot known as Perfect Park. The EOC's existing building at 976 Embarcadero Del Mar is at the middle-right, showing a proposed expansion. The project was rejected by the County Planning Commission but approved on appeal by the board of supervisors under the leadership of Supervisor Bill Wallace, a former resident of Isla Vista. In 1991, Isla Vista voters approved a plan for the Isla Vista Park District to purchase the property and create an official park at the historic site. The Park District paid the church about $1.5 million for the property, which the EOC had purchased for about $250,000. Isla Vista *Free Press* graphic.

In early 1988, the EOC threw down the gauntlet to those who considered Perfect Park a significant relic of Isla Vista's history by submitting plans to the County for a new two-story, 19,000-square-foot building on Perfect Park. The move sparked an all-out war that lasted several years.

building on Perfect Park. The move sparked an all-out war that lasted several years.

Under a lot of pressure from the public, the Isla Vista Park Board quickly invited the EOC to consider a trade for other properties the District owned on which to build their new temple. The church initially seemed interested in the Del Sol Vernal Pool Preserve, an 11-acre parcel along Camino Corto Road at El Colegio Road. Because of the vernal pools on the property, and because of a substantial grant received by the park district from the State Coastal Conservancy to preserve the vernal pools, it was highly unlikely that such a trade was feasible.

The Park Board suggested trading the EOC's present building and all of Perfect Park for a large parcel it owned along Estero Road at Camino Corto and on several occasions during Park Board meetings asked the church to consider this trade. However, the church refused to participate in any negotiations. A spokesman for the church later said that they hadn't considered such talk seriously because they had never received a

2008 photo of the property along Estero Road that was offered by the Isla Vista Park District in trade for the EOC's property known as Perfect Park in the center of town. The church rejected the trade and won approval from the County supervisors on appeal from the planning commission to build a two-and-one-half story, 16,000-square-foot building on their property.

County Planning Commissioner Ed Maschke led the commission in rejecting the EOC's plans to build in Perfect Park, stating bluntly that they preferred the trade option offered by the Isla Vista Park District. Isla Vista *Free Press* photograph.

written offer from the I. V. Park District.

In October 1988, the board of supervisors voted to return the project to the applicant, suggesting that it be scaled down. Revised plans showed a 16,000-square-foot building, called Phase Two, with a 1,200-square-foot addition to the present building and 61 parking spaces to be built on Perfect Park as part of Phase One. Both phases were later turned down by the County's planning commission, because of the traffic impacts and because the commissioners felt a trade for the Estero property was a much better idea.

In expressing the commission's unanimous opposition to the project,

Commissioner Michael Bennett stated: "For many years, the community has expressed its wish that it (Perfect Park) be held in open space as some kind of park . . . . I'm very uncomfortable taking this last centerpiece of open space in Isla Vista and putting anything on it, whether it be a church or a shopping center . . . . If the community is unwilling to come up to the line and say yes — we're going to compensate, we're going to trade in a way satisfactory (to the church) — then I would consider it (the church project)."

And the community had stepped up to offer such a trade.

However, on appeal, the County Board of Supervisors on November 21, 1988 voted unanimously to approve Phase One of the project (including the 61 parking spaces in Perfect Park), and most expressed strong support for Phase Two, although they delayed final consideration of the second phase until a later date.

Fred Clough, the EOC's high-priced attorney, addressing the County board of supervisors during the church's successful appeal of their building project on their property known as Perfect Park. Isla Vista *Free Press* photograph.

To the disgust of many observers, the supervisors, under the leadership of Bill Wallace, approved both phases of the project being constructed without a full environmental impact report, which would have forced the church to consider a trade with the Isla Vista Park District.

County Supervisor Bill Wallace speaking in favor of the EOC's building plans at a December 1990 meeting of the board of supervisors. Isla Vista *Free Press* photograph.

Most people close to the situation were flabbergasted by the approval. This was a new board of supervisors, sworn in earlier that same month, that had five so-called "environmentalists" on it. And why was Wallace supporting the project after years of battling the very politically active EOC on growth issues?

Wallace never publicly stated why he supported the church, which was especially unusual given that his Planning Commissioner Ed Maschke, one of his best personally friends, had so eloquently opposed it. Other people close to Wallace, however, suggested it was payback for I.V. Park Board member Mike Boyd having run for supervisor against him in 1988 -- a campaign that had little support in the community and was editorially opposed by the Isla Vista *Free Press*.

Although Isla Vista voters continued to support Wallace for supervisor against pro-growth opponents for another two elections, his support of the EOC project pretty much alienated Isla Vista's activists from the former Isla Vistan.

Accordingly, the 61-space parking lot that still scars Perfect Park is popularly known as the Bill Wallace Memorial Parking Lot.

The Committee to Save Perfect Park

As the chilling news spread through town, a committee formed calling themselves "The Committee to Save Perfect Park." The group, which included this author, quickly set about gathering signatures on a petition opposing the project for presentation to the supervisors when they met again

The EOC building in the left-foreground, with the Bill Wallace Memorial Parking Lot off to the right and Perfect Park in the distance (center).

to finalize their approval. Close to 2,000 signatures were gathered in a little over two weeks, plus the Associated Students Legislative Council voted 13-2 to oppose the project. However, the Supervisors unanimously approved the project in January 1990.

The church quickly dispatched bulldozers to construct the parking lot needed for the project. Dozens of people gathered to watch the event. As the bulldozers roared, two members of the Committee to Save Perfect Park, Scott Wexler and Rob Puddicombe, climbed into the new trenches, sitting down in front of the menacing machines. Although this temporarily halted their progress, police soon appeared to handcuff the protesters and haul them off to the local police station where they were ticketed for, ironically, disturbing the peace.

The focus of efforts to save Perfect Park quickly turned to the Isla Vista Park Board where there was a wobbly 3-2 majority opposing the EOC's plans. The committee soon drew up a referendum petition requiring the board to use their powers of eminent domain to condemn the property in favor of building a park there. The measure went on the ballot in June 1991.

The NO campaign was particularly vicious. The EOC spent thousands of dollars on advertising in the UCSB *Daily Nexus*. One cartoon showed the EOC families being driven out of town depicted as Jews being stuffed into boxcars on their way to the gas chambers.

Lacking such resources, the YES campaign relied on door-to-door talking to voters and a lot of hand-painted posters.

The referendum requiring the Park District to purchase the property passed handily, but only after Isla Vista Park Board member Mike Boyd pointed out to County election officials that they had mistakenly run ballots through their computer from another measure strongly opposed by Isla Vista voters for several precincts in the Perfect Park race.

> *The referendum requiring the park district to purchase the property passed handily, but only after Isla Vista Park Board member Mike Boyd pointed out to County election officials that they had mistakenly run ballots through their computer from another measure strongly opposed by Isla Vista voters for several precincts in the Perfect Park race.*

The Park District reportedly paid the EOC close to $1.5 million for Perfect Park, roughly six times what they purchased it for originally. This was the first and only time in its 36-year history (1972-2008) that the Park District used its power to condemn property, having bought roughly 30 properties through the years without it.

The EOC used the money to buy property in Goleta for a future church site, and they recently secured a required zoning change on the property to complete their plans. Meanwhile, they continue to hold church ceremonies and events at their 976 Embarcadero del Mar site, although most of its member families have moved to Goleta and are no longer politically active.

What is particularly galling to Perfect Park supporters is that the 61-space parking lot, built as part of the EOC's Phase One, is still there. Despite being owned by the Park District, it's under lease to the EOC.

Perfect Park, Finally

In April 1995, 75 volunteers showed up to plant hundreds of native plants in Perfect Park as it assumed its current appearance of rolling hills.

In May 1995 a group of current and former residents of Isla Vista, including this author, asked the Isla Vista Park Board to establish a design contest for a proper monument in Perfect Park to the international anti-war movement of 1965-75. The monument was to be the first of its kind to commemorate the peaceful struggle against the war in Vietnam. The board instead established a committee of proponents and opponents to review the concept of such a memorial.

Bob Potter, UCSB Professor of Theater Arts, assumed the leadership of the committee, although he was physically threatened by anonymous phone calls. Indeed, Ben Roberts, a former CIA

provocateur in Laos, notorious Isla Vista landlord, and a member of the Park District's committee, publicly threatened to blow up the monument if it ever was constructed.

After two months of acrimonious meetings and no compromises, the park board disbanded this committee and formed the Perfect Park Monument Implementation Committee (PPMIC). The park board also approved the placement of such a monument in Perfect Park but stated flatly that no Park District resources were to be used in building it.

The monument to the worldwide anti-war movement in Isla Vista's Perfect Park was dedicated on June 10, 2003.

The goal of the PPMIC was to raise $25,000 and to conduct an international search for an artist to

Perfect Park in 2008 with the monument to the worldwide anti-war movement in the background.

design and build the monument. Although it took several years, the monument, which was designed and built by Santa Barbara artist Colin Firth, was dedicated on June 10, 2003, exactly 33 years from the famous sit-in of 1970 in Perfect Park that resulted in 390 people being arrested (see Chapter 2). The plaque reads simply:

"In a spirit of remembrance, inspiration and reconciliation, we commemorate the people who worked for peace, justice and nonviolence in Isla Vista and elsewhere during the

Vietnam war era."

While there are many monuments to the warriors of the Vietnam War era, the monument to the peace movement in Isla Vista's Perfect Park is thought to be the only one of its kind anywhere.

At the commemoration event, PPMIC Chair Bob Potter, playwright, then-UCSB professor, and co-author of <u>The Campus by the Sea Where the Bank Burned Down</u>, a 1970 report to the President's Commission on Campus Unrest, gave the opening address, which began:

A third of a century ago, our forefathers…and foremothers — and fore-motherfuckers—hippies and yippies; speed freaks and Jesus freaks; Students radicalized by their professors; Professors radicalized by their students; Anarchists, Pacifists and Registered Republicans; Flower Children, Franciscan Friars and pissed-off Football Players; Marxist-Leninists and Proto-Feminists; Surfers, Sorority Sisters and Sexual Revolutionaries; Space Cadets and Vietnam Vets; the Hare Krishna and the Woodstock Nation; Visionaries in all

Bob Potter, UCSB professor and chair of the Perfect Mark Monument Implementation Committee, giving the dedication speech on June 10, 2003. Robert Bernstein photograph.

The wording on the plaque in the center of the monument reads:

In a spirit of remembrance, inspiration and reconciliation, we commemorate the people who worked for peace, justice and nonviolence in Isla Vista and elsewhere during the Vietnam war era.

colors and Mindblown lead guitarists of non-existent bands; not to mention winos, transients, alcoholics Anonymous and Otherwise, the Chairman of the Sociology Department, and ordinary college students caught up in the pure adrenaline of the moment —

All of these people, and indescribable hundreds more, made history with their asses, by sitting down on them here in Perfect Park, in violation of a Police Curfew Order, linking arms to defend their community.

The full text of Potter's speech is found in Appendix B.

The EOC in Retrospect

In summary, the EOC is not insidious, but it is organized. Their influence in Isla Vista (and Goleta) was immense for awhile. Their penchant to run for public office and to speak at public hearings made them much different than other churches in the area. In fact, in many ways they were a political action committee.

Yet, it is difficult to talk about this side of their activities because, as one of their political opponents said in the 1987 Goleta Water Board race, "You can't talk about the church connection between Lewis and McFarland in the campaign because people will call you religious bigots."

In this regard, the EOC certainly had the best of both worlds for awhile. But they didn't win every battle.

ADDENDUM

In the spring of 2008, the EOC sold its church building and property in Isla Vista to the County of Santa Barbara (Isla Vista Redevelopment Agency -- IVRDA) for a reported $1.875 million. The EOC has a two-year lease on their existing building and is in construction on a new church in Goleta.

The IVRDA also purchased the I.V. Medical Clinic building at the same time for a reported $2.6 million. The clinic, part of the Santa Barbara Neighborhood Clinics, has a ten-year lease, with an opt out if/ when they find another suitable location in Isla Vista.

The IVRDA plans to raze both structures and pursue the acquisition of subterranean rights to Perfect Park and People's Park from the Isla Vista Park District and build an underground parking lot under the four properties. Furthermore, the IVRDA would then grant back the surface rights to these four properties to the Isla Vista Park District, with sufficient funding to rebuild a major park.

In 1990, the County supervisors established the IVRDA with an appointed project advisory committee (PAC) to present the board with a Master Plan. The EIR on it was certified in 2007 and the Master Plan was approved by the County board of supervisors shortly thereafter. However, this Master Plan was rejected by the State Coastal Commission, reportedly because of parking issues in the downtown area.

Under existing policies, the Isla Vista Park District cannot sell or trade properties it owns without first a 2/3-vote of the electorate. Accordingly, the I.V. Park Board majority has put on the November 2008 ballot a proposition (Measure D) that, if it passes, would authorize the board of directors, with a 2/3-vote of the board (practically speaking, it would require a 4/5-vote of the five-member board), to sell or trade several district-owned properties.

Specifically, Measure D asks:

    Shall a measure be approved to authorize:

    (i) the sale or trade of Pardall Gardens and the District office properties; and

(ii) the transfer and/or swap of subterranean or other use rights from Anisq'Oyo, People's and Perfect parks?

Any funds realized shall only be used for a community center and District infrastructure. These authorizations shall expire ten (10) years following the effective date of this measure.

A person of goodwill would assume that (a) Anisq'Oyo Park is included here only to give a super-majority of the board some options regarding the future of Anisq'Oyo Park without the expense of another ballot measure, and (b) additional funds are needed to build a community center.

A skeptical person might wonder if there is some hidden agenda behind the inclusion of Anisq'Oyo Park in this proposition, what "other use rights" might include, and what the use of surplus funds from these trades/sales for "District infrastructure" projects might include.

Because Measure D requires a 2/3-vote of the electorate at the November 2008 election, and because most of the nine candidates vying for three open seats on the Isla Vista Park Board at the same election are actively opposing Measure D's passage, it's very likely its passage will fail.

In addition, in late September 2008, the lead County staff person on the Isla Vista Master Plan resigned, leaving the situation in turmoil because he was the major advocate of the park swap and underground parking lot.

Into this vacuum, some activists have raised the possibility of working with the County to keep the Isla Vista Medical Clinic Building intact and remodel it for use as the town's community center instead of the planned community center on Estero Road. This much less expensive option has a lot of merit, but doesn't deal with the parking issue in downtown Isla Vista.

-- C.L. October 2008

CHAPTER 13

POLICING ISLA VISTA

The Man Behind the Badge

John Carpenter was the sheriff of Santa Barbara County from 1970 through 1990, a long time for any elected official in these parts. Before that he was the chief of an eight-member police force in Carpinteria, not a very impressive position from which to launch a successful campaign for a countywide office.

But in 1970, the incumbent sheriff had lost a lot of credibility for his handling of the civil disturbances in Isla Vista and Carpenter swept to an easy victory over the incumbent's endorsed successor. So it could be said that Isla Vista had a lot to do with Carpenter becoming sheriff — in a strange kind of way.

Carpenter kept the Foot Patrol going in Isla Vista and had it report monthly to the meetings of the Isla Vista Community Council until it went dormant in 1987. On several occasions while seeking re-

Sheriff John Carpenter was swept into office in 1970 on a reform platform following general public disgust at the way police handled the civil disturbances in Isla Vista earlier that year. 1988 Isla Vista *Free Press* photo.

election, Carpenter endorsed Isla Vista having its own city, or at least he said that I.V.'s residents could adequately handle being in charge of a police force in a City of Isla Vista.

Through the years, Carpenter's relationship with Isla Vista was fairly decent, even though two write-in campaigns against him were launched from I.V. — in 1974 by Larry Padway and in 1978 by Mark Fontana. Padway's campaign drew over 1,500 votes countywide and almost forced Carpenter into a run-off with another candidate. And while Fontana's was less successful, it was a lot more fun.

Fontana for Sheriff

Fontana's campaign platform had three planks. The planks were stated humorously, but each contained more than a kernel of truth.

Fontana called for a drug enforcement plan that would bust only the big dealers — especially the Sheriff's Narcotics Task Force. It seems that some officers from this immensely unpopular special unit had been caught stealing captured cocaine and selling it back onto the street.

Secondly, Fontana called for no enforcement of the law against nude sunbathing. At the time, there were three popular nude beaches in southern Santa Barbara County, including Coal Oil Point on West Campus.

Thirdly, he wanted to make the jails safe for prisoners — two inmates had been killed or committed suicide under suspicious circumstances in the year running up to the election. In addition, several other prisoners had been beaten either by inmates or jailers — it wasn't clear who.

Fontana's campaign poster showed him with a vest and a ten-gallon cowboy hat, with a sheriff's badge from the Old West drawn on his lapel. Despite what most Isla Vistans thought was a great campaign, Fontana won only a thousand votes countywide and didn't push Carpenter as he won his third term handily.

The sheriff was able to keep his sense of humor about these write-in campaigns. Much better

A poster urging voters to write in Mark Fontana for Sheriff in 1978.

than his deputies did, in fact. The Deputy Sheriff's Association wouldn't let either Padway or Fontana speak at their endorsement forums. After the election, Carpenter disbanded the narc squad, only tokenly enforced the nude beach ordinance, and cleaned up the jail situation.

Antiwar Demonstrations at the Santa Barbara Airport

In May of 1972, Carpenter faced perhaps his most difficult decision up to that point in office, especially given the role that the antiwar demonstrations of 1970 had played in his election.

A rally of more than 7,000 people had materialized around noon on campus on the lawn leading down to the lagoon behind the UCen following some action by the Nixon-Kissinger team. I think it was a restart of bombing of North Vietnam, but I'm not sure of the details any more.

After the speakers finished, people rose from the audience to recommend what concrete steps should be taken in response to the bombing. Most suggestions were politely ignored or laughed off. Finally, Jim Gregory, then a writer for the Santa Barbara News & Review, the local progressive weekly, offered a plan that immediately rang true. He suggested that everyone march to the Santa Barbara Municipal Airport and sit-in on the runway as a symbolic protest to the U.S. air attack. People nodded, began clapping, and turned to each other saying, "Yes! That's it!"

I'd never seen such a spontaneous agreement on the part of a large crowd — outside of a sporting event.

[The speaker] suggested that everyone march to the Santa Barbara Municipal Airport and sit-in on the runway as a symbolic protest to the U.S. air attack. People nodded, began clapping, and turned to each other saying, "Yes! That's it!"

I'd never seen such a spontaneous agreement on the part of a large crowd — outside of a sporting event.

The march started immediately. At least 4,000 people walked up Los Carneros Road, turned east on Hollister Avenue and onto the airport runway. The crowd was warned by airport authorities to leave immediately, but no one paid attention to them. Someone gathered some logs and a bonfire was started in the middle of the runway. The crowd was chanting the anti-war slogans of the time: "The People, united, will never be defeated." And my personal favorite: "Two-Four-Six-Eight — Nixon Eats Shit."

Suddenly a dozen black and white police cars appeared at the end of the runway, perhaps a half-mile away from the crowd. As they began driving slowly toward us, the heat from their engines invoked a wavy hallucination.

After about an hour, a big yellow school bus filled with police pulled onto the airport grounds. A jeep appeared, with Carpenter at the helm, and began circling the runway that held the demonstrators. With a huge megaphone, Carpenter shouted that everyone should leave within five minutes or he would "clear the area." While no one knew exactly what "clearing the area" meant, it sounded pretty painful to this demonstrator.

Suddenly a dozen black and white police cars appeared at the end of the runway, perhaps a half-mile away from the crowd. As they began driving slowly toward us, the heat from their engines evoked a wavy hallucination.

At least half the people — being mostly sane — jumped up and fled back toward Hollister Ave. I don't mind admitting that I moved from my seat in the center of the crowd over toward the edge of those who remained. But, at least 2,000 people held strong on the runway, which gave me enough courage to sit back down.

As the black and whites got about halfway up the runway toward us, Carpenter called them off. He wasn't going to have his men attack this crowd of unarmed demonstrators.

He had given us the runway.

Boy were we happy! We remained there for several hours, burning fires, singing revolutionary songs, huddling together, and cheering wildly at the announcement that all flights had been cancelled for the rest of the day.

At sunset we marched back to I.V. and partied way into the night in the vacant lots of what now is Anisq'Oyo Park. While most of the marchers celebrated, the more radical leadership met in small groups around town where they decided there should be an attempt to take over U.S. 101 the next morning. Word spread quickly and a caravan crept out of Isla Vista at dawn.

But Carpenter was having none of this. As thirty or forty cars moved onto U.S. 101 from the Ward Memorial Drive on-ramp, they found it blocked. Suddenly Sheriff's deputies appeared on foot and walked along the highway banging the trapped cars with their night sticks, creating a lot of dents and even breaking some windows. Most people backed out quickly but some were forced to leave their cars and were chased on foot by deputies most of the way back to I.V.

A Second Chance

Two years later, an antiwar march down State Street in Santa Barbara had to cross U.S. 101 at the traffic lights in order to get to the beach area. Some three or four thousand people were in the march and it was a pretty high-spirited event. As the crowd crossed 101 under the protection of Sheriff's deputies, a veteran of the attempted takeover of 101 in 1972 shouted: "Everybody sit down — we've finally got 101!"

Well, everybody did. We began chanting, locking arms together, and hooting those eerie high-pitched war hoops adopted from the Arabs fighting the French during the Algerian revolution.

> *As the crowd crossed 101 under the protection of Sheriff's deputies, a veteran of the attempted takeover of 101 in 1972 shouted: "Everybody sit down — we've finally got 101!"*

The Sheriff let us sit for about 20 minutes, but when the Sunday afternoon traffic got backed up five miles in each direction, one of the deputies began banging a metal utility pole with his nightstick. Another collective thought process struck the crowd, because almost at once, everyone rose and began walking again toward the beach.

Carpenter had let us have the highway for a few minutes — perhaps so we could feel that we had accomplished something — and then fulfilled his responsibility by moving us out.

A smart man. Maybe even a caring man.

Sometime later I spoke to him about these two events. He told me that he had a son who was just coming of draft age and he understood what we were trying to say in our rambunctious efforts. He didn't say he agreed with us — he just said he could empathize with us.

Shortly after this conversation, Carpenter announced he would retire at the end of his term in 1990. I wished him well.

The Isla Vista Foot Patrol

by Andrew Shulman

Andrew Shulman was a UCSB student and aspiring journalist. This story appeared in the May 17, 1988 Isla Vista Free Press.

When you walk into the Foot Patrol office at 6547 Pardall Road, you realize immediately that it isn't the ordinary kind of police station.

First of all, the person who greets you smiles and the atmosphere is definitely laid back. Secondly, there is a poster on the wall of the Isla Vista branch of the Bank of America in flames — a reminder of the event that lead to the establishment of the Foot Patrol.

A foot-and-bike patrol created in the fall of 1970, the Foot Patrol is the main policing force in a town that has 10% of the population of the county's unincorporated areas but 25% of its reported crimes. The Foot Patrol was designed as a solution to the specific problems Isla Vista was experiencing in the wake of the 1970 civil disturbances — problems, some said, that were directly associated with the lack of community relations between police and students.

But there were problems in the beginning bridging that gap — some of which have not entirely gone away.

The Isla Vista Foot Patrol office at 6547 Pardall Rd. in 1988. Half Sheriff-funded, half UCSB-funded, the Foot Patrol has been in existence since 1970. Isla Vista *Free Press* photograph.

Early Days

In the early 1970s, military policemen near the end of their tours of duty in Vietnam were offered early discharges if they agreed to join law enforcement agencies upon their return to the United States. Several former MPs found themselves on the Isla Vista Foot Patrol and the result was an intensification of the sense of alienation between the police and the community that existed during the riots.

One resident recalled Foot Patrol officers referring to Isla Vista residents in that period as "gooks." In return, mistrust of the newly formed Foot Patrol felt by the community was echoed in the nicknames residents had for them: "authoritarian pigs," "Nazi punks," and "the army of the establishment."

In the early years, the Foot Patrol program was made possible by a grant from the California Council on

The new Foot Patrol Office at 6504 Trigo Rd., which opened in September 2008. This Sheriff's patrol car is parked in a red-curb zone in front of a fire hydrant.

Criminal Justice, the state agency in charge of disbursing funds from the federal Anti-Crime and Safe Streets Act of 1968.

Then as now, the UCSB Police Department assigns six officers to the patrol on an 18-month rotational basis and the Santa Barbara County Sheriffs Department provides six of its deputies. In this way, the financing has become split between the County and UCSB.

The Foot Patrol operates between 7:30 AM and 3:00 AM, with auto patrols covering the remaining hours. Even during the regular shift, some of the patrol work is still done with the Sheriff's black-and-whites and the University's all white cars.

Santa Barbara County Sheriff John Carpenter maintains that the current goals of the Foot Patrol are no different from its original objectives — to humanize the relationship between police and Isla Vista residents and to help stifle the area's extraordinary crime rate.

"Nothing has changed in respect to the objectives of the Foot Patrol," said Carpenter. "What has changed is the constituency. Current Isla Vista residents are very different from who they were back then."

A unique feature of the patrol, and one that has attracted great interest nationwide, is the return to what was once a basic trademark of all police activities — the foot officer on the beat. The Houston Police Department recently adopted a similar "community policing" program, assigning each officer a permanent neighborhood beat. Different variations of community policing have been seen in Dallas, Baltimore, and Los Angeles. But the I.V. Foot Patrol was one of the first.

One problem, however, is that the Foot Patrol was originally designed as a "specially trained" force of officers. Patrolmen received special community relations training, including public relations, human relations, race and ethnic relations, and

1988 CRIME STATISTICS in Isla Vista

Note: Isla Vista's population of 15,000 (excluding the UCSB Campus) is approximately 10% of the jurisdiction of the County Sheriff.

OFFENSES	Total	% change vs.1987	% of total County
All felonies	563	+38	15
All Misdemeanors	4,276	+11	35
County Ordinances (open containers, leash law, etc)	857	+14	51
All assaults	143	+17	23
Felony Sex	10	-2	91
Rape	9	+450	28
Burglary	310	+28	19
Theft (including bikes)	845	-20	34
Liquor	1,863	+13	52
Traffic, moving	473	+72	10
Traffic, parking	4,937	+69	62

SOURCE: Sgt. Sam Gross, Co. Sheriff Dept.

Note: I spent six weeks talking with the responsible parties in the Santa Barbara County Sheriff's Department in an attempt to get comparable crime statistics to the 1988 data for 1978, 1998, and 2007. This is the standard format used locally and statewide. I was recently told I would have to wait another month, which was beyond the publication date for this book. In 1989, Sgt. Sam Gross was able to get the data for 1988 overnight. -- *CL*

sensitivity sessions with Isla Vista residents. Currently, however, officers assigned to the Foot Patrol do not receive any of the special training needed to help them deal with problems unique to the Isla Vista community.

However, both the UCSB Police Department and the Santa Barbara County Sheriff's Department claim their officers receive specialized training in all aspects of law enforcement before they are ever assigned to the Foot Patrol, with each County-supplied deputy "handpicked" and personally approved by the Sheriff himself. The assumption is that the kind of community relations training, which I.V.'s special police force received during the 1970s, has become generalized in all police training schools.

MacPherson. And serving on the Foot Patrol is now a priority among police officers. According to Lt. Joseph Smith, special details with the Sheriff's Department, deputies wishing to work on the

Foot Patrol must pass an intensive screening process. "Every officer who comes to the Foot Patrol is handpicked for a wide variety of personal qualities and the good job they've done with the department," said Smith. "Proof of that can be seen in the absolute absence of complaints against Foot Patrol officers despite the much greater number of calls they receive as compared to those assigned to the main station."

One of the reasons there are so few complaints against the Foot Patrol most certainly is the difficulty of obtaining an official complaint form. While the UCSB police chief quickly produced a university form upon request, several days of search at both the Foot Patrol office and the Sheriff's Department produced only evasive answers. The most certain thing, however, is that you can't find one at the Foot Patrol office.

Even though all police officers may now receive "community relations" training at

One of the reasons there are so few complaints against the Foot Patrol most certainly is the difficulty of obtaining an official complaint form. While the UCSB police chief quickly produced a university form upon request, several days of search at both the Foot Patrol office and the Sheriff's Department produced only evasive answers. The most certain thing, however, is that you can't find one at the Foot Patrol office.

the police academy, there is still a concern that Foot Patrol officers should receive training that is specifically relevant to the problems currently found in Isla Vista. The concern is illustrated in the criticism voiced by some Isla Vista residents.

Unidentified young man being questioned and ID'd on the sidewalk in front of the Isla Vista Market. Isla Vista *Free Press* photograph.

"They seem to go out of their way to harass people," said one 17-year-old resident who said he's been brought into the Foot Patrol office for questioning six times without being charged with a crime.

"Once they get to know someone, they automatically start hassling him," he said.

This same person has friends who allegedly have been beaten up with nightsticks far beyond any need to restrain them for questioning. These incidents go unreported because the youths are afraid of retribution later.

"After all, we have to live here," he concluded.

Many women have complained that Foot Patrol officers were not doing their part to limit the kinds of sexual abuse during Isla Vista's Halloween celebrations of the last few officer years. In 1987, a citizens committee called "Red Alert" was initiated to perform much of that function. While the Red Alert people felt that they had accomplished quite a bit, the head of the Foot Patrol at the time dismissed their efforts as "relatively harmless."

Cheri Gerse of the UCSB Women's Center says that her staff provides training to UCSB officers regarding rape prevention and sensitivity, while the Santa Barbara Rape Crisis Center does much the same for the Sheriff's Department.

Dumpster Burning. It's not that policing Isla Vista is all that easy. It's not unusual to come across a dumpster fire on a Saturday night. The torching of junked couches in the middle of the street used to be a regular springtime ritual. In fact, for a couple of years there was a popular band called "Burning Couches" that regularly played the Anisq'Oyo Park Amphitheater. Isla Vista *Free Press* photograph.

"While I've found that the officers are very professional in their investigative capacity, some handle our sensitivity training better than others," Gerse told the *Free Press*. "It depends a lot on what's going on in their personal lives."

Rape is always under-reported to law enforcement agencies. Gerse says that there are probably 10 to 20 times more rapes than ever get reported. "We did a study recently that indicated there are between three and ten date rapes each week on just the campus properties," she said.

The Foot Patrol has not gone without its share of public embarrassment either. In 1983, a formal complaint was filed against members of the Foot Patrol by the Phi Sigma Kappa fraternity alleging that several off-duty officers fired bottle rockets and threw firecrackers at the fraternity's house on Cordova Road. The complaint also stated that the officers were drinking beer inside the Foot Patrol office and continued to shoot off the fireworks despite receiving complaints from members of

FOOT PATROL Continued on page 139

HALLOWEEN

Halloween is the second most popular holiday in the United States. But it's definitely #1 in Isla Vista. Starting sometime in the 1960s, locals began dressing up and attending keg parties along Del Playa Drive. In the '70s the parties moved in land, too, and area high schoolers began

sneaking in. But in the '80s, things really heated up after *Playboy* magazine named UCSB a top party school and noted the bacchanalian flavor Halloween had taken on. All hell broke loose in 1986 when over 30,000 people showed up, literally thousands arriving in a fleet of chartered busses from San Diego State University. The town was a madhouse; you literally had to yell to hear yourself heard to a person

These students probably won't write home about their expressive costumes. Isla Vista *Free Press* photographs by Keith Madigan.

Halloween party in the middle of Del Playa Dr.

standing next to you as far inland as Abrego Rd. The cops busted over 1,000 persons that weekend, nearly three-fourths from SDSU. The next year, UC officials advertised at other California campuses "Don't Come to I.V." and police shut down all non-resident traffic entering I.V. on Halloween night. Community leaders reluctantly joined this campaign to keep the event strictly local, which has more-or-less worked through the years.

-- *C.L.*

The morning after on Del Playa Drive.

FOOT PATROL, *continued from page 137*

the fraternity.

Race is another issue in Isla Vista that seldom is handled in a manner satisfactory to minorities. In the fall of 1987, someone broke into a black person's apartment, stole his computer and other items, and spray-painted racial slurs on the walls. This was reported by the Foot Patrol as simply a theft.

In late 1987, a black woman was hit by a large rock thrown by a fraternity member as she worked in the street near the fraternity house. The police never uncovered the identity of the person throwing the rock because they permitted the fraternity brothers to hide him in the house. A follow up investigation by the Greek Peer Review Board got buried in UCSB Vice-Chancellor Edward Birch's office.

One long-term resident remembers when the Foot Patrol officers would spend a day each year in a retreat with community leaders at the University's Cliff House on West Campus.

Sgt. James Drinkwater in front of the Isla Vista Foot Patrol Office when it was still at 6547 Pardall Rd. Isla Vista *Free Press* photograph.

"These were great opportunities both for us to get to know the police better, but for them to get to know us, too. I'm sorry that this kind of interaction has been dropped," he said.

There is, however, strong support for the Foot Patrol from many I.V. residents and business owners. Verne Johnson, owner of the Isla Vista Market, enthusiastically supports them. "I.V. would be 100 times worse a place without them," he said. "I think that they're great."

One young mother, who asked not to be identified, said that, "They have always been very helpful and very concerned when we've had any problems."

In 1976, the Isla Vista Community Council (IVCC) invented an award called "The Turkey of the Month" in order to call attention to one Foot Patrol officer who most people thought spent too much time harassing residents. This prestigious award was given to UCSB Officer Al Phillips for having made so many marijuana arrests. A member of the Foot Patrol confided that he thought

Phillips made far more than half of all the arrests for small amounts of marijuana possession in the entire county.

Other members of the Foot Patrol must have had some empathy with what the IVCC was expressing with its tongue-in-cheek award, because they framed the certificate and kept it hung on the wall at the Foot Patrol Office for several years.

Beginning in 1972, the Foot Patrol reported at least once a month to public meetings of the IVCC, relating crime stats for the previous period and discussing any event or policing policy within legal limits. With the phase out of the IVCC in 1987, this regular reporting to the community no longer occurs.

However, Sgt. James Drinkwater and Lt. Joe Smith, both of the Sheriff's Department, often attend the monthly meetings of the Isla Vista Federation [see pages 169-70] and the UCSB Major Events Committee. Both are good opportunities for interaction, but in a more limited fashion.

Drinkwater reported recently at a Federation meeting that he and his staff were stepping up their ticketing of illegally parked cars. One community member suggested that the police should warn the community of such a change in policy, because most people have grown used to the lax enforcement. "It would be better to start out with an education campaign in the fall, and begin a strong ticketing plan right away, rather than waiting until after Christmas," he said.

While the officers reacted somewhat defensively at the meeting ("People complain both when we do it and when we don't!"), the stronger enforcement plan appears to have at least leveled off in the past couple of weeks.

May 4, 1989 Community Meeting of Residents and Police

Officers: "We Get Scared Out There Sometimes."

Residents: "Police Don't Show Us Respect."

This report first appeared as an article in the Isla Vista Free Press *in May 1989.*

On Thursday, May 4th, 1989 the leadership of the Isla Vista Food Patrol sat down with about sixty residents, the press, and a couple of administrators from UCSB to talk about a widely perceived deterioration in police/community relations in Isla Vista.

UCSB Police Chief John MacPherson (left) and Sheriff's Patrol Division Captain Ed Pecino at the May 4, 1989 meeting with residents. Isla Vista *Free Press* photograph.

At the front table was UCSB Police Chief John MacPherson and the Sheriff's Patrol Division Captain Ed Pecino, as well as the former head of the Foot Patrol Sgt. James Drinkwater, and Sgt. Fred Olguin, who had succeeded Drinkwater just a week before.

The crowd included the community's top elected leadership — several members of the Isla Vista Park Board and the UCSB Associated Students Legislative Council, including newly-elected A.S. President Mike Stowers and outgoing Vice-President Ellen Thornton. Conspicuous in his absence was County Supervisor Bill Wallace, himself an I.V. resident. Wallace stated later that he was out of town.

The meeting had been arranged by UCSB Ombudsperson Geoffry Wallace, because, as he said, "Everyone at the University is concerned that I.V. has the right kind of policing."

Scott Wexler, a long-time I.V. resident, started off the dialogue. "Living in I.V., you make adjustments, and the police have to make adjustments, too. You can't just go strictly by the book, and lately there's been too much enforcement by the book."

[One resident stated that he] felt that it was unnecessary for the Foot Patrol and backups from other areas to wear riot gear on weekend patrols. [Sheriff's Patrol Division Captain Ed Pecino responded that] they dress appropriately, "which unfortunately, often means we dress expecting violence."

Wexler also felt that it was unnecessary for the Foot Patrol and backups from other areas to wear riot gear on weekend patrols.

"There are too many times when there is a basic lack of respect on the part of officers toward I.V. residents, especially students. Too often the police are a blunt instrument of authority. There is a basic lack of willingness to deal with students on an equal basis. And this just repeats the cycle even more."

DAN ZUMWINKLE
Associated Students Leg. Council

Mike Lupro stated that there was a lot more serious crimes than loud parties, and why couldn't the police de-emphasize shutting down parties that are only disturbing a few people, while benefitting hundreds in some cases.

Pecino responded that he agreed there was a problem, but that "We have very little discretion. If we receive a compliant about a loud party, for instance, we have to respond."

Pecino stated that many of these problems are community problems, not police ones, and they needed to be dealt with by the community. "But, don't ask us to ignore laws—we just can't do it," he said. And as far as what they wear was concerned, he said they dress appropriately, "which unfortunately, often means we dress expecting violence."

Several persons questioned the general attitude of Foot Patrol and back-up officers toward residents, especially students. "There is a definite need for dialogue between the community and police," said Mike Stowers. "It's gotten to be a moral question."

"There are too many times when there is a basic lack of respect on the part of officers toward I.V. residents, especially students," said Dan Zumwinkle, who based his opinion on his four years of experience in student government, as an R.A. in the dorm, and as a student manager. "Too often the police are a blunt instrument of authority. There is a basic lack of willingness to deal with students on an equal basis. And this just repeats the cycle even more."

Marc Villa, outgoing A.S. Leg. Council representative, said, "In my four years of student life here, I've found that most police interaction (towards students) is negative. There needs to be more of a dialogue."

Scott Abbott, assistant administrator at the Park District, noted that, "I've noticed in just the last few weeks that there has been a basic change of attitude on the part of police. With my job I've had a lot of interaction with the Foot Patrol, and it has always been very friendly, on a first name basis. But recently, officers are giving very short, defensive answers to my questions. It's definitely different."

A man and his dog in Anisq'Oyo Park. Foot Patrol officers ticketing this I.V. resident and confiscating his dog for being off its leash on a sunny afternoon. Isla Vista *Free Press* photo.

Heather Hewson, also a member of the Park District's staff, went even further. "I have to say it's definitely an antagonistic approach [by the police]. At the last few events in the [Anisq'Oyo] Park, there's been a lot more police. It's just harassment. While people are in the park, their homes might be being robbed. Why are the police concentrating their enforcement efforts in the park at that time?"

Park Board representative Mike Boyd also complained that police seem to be concentrating on enforcement activities in Anisq'Oyo Park. "The park is supposed to be a place where people can get away from their overcrowded apartments," he said. "But now its becoming intimidating to go to the Park. There's even a lot of leash law enforcement now during events. I can't believe that this is what the community wants."

Pecino's response to most of these comments was that the police have to put up with "a lot of crap" in Isla Vista. "We want people to understand that we get scared sometimes in situations in I.V."

"When officers go to some of these parties in I.V., with hundreds of people on the street, drinking, we're scared, and we want to protect ourselves," he continued. "We've had a couple of deputies beat up, one was bitten, another had a gun drawn on him last week. I'd like to see more of you walk the streets with a Foot Patrol officer. They're subject to this kind of garbage every night."

Also, Pecino pointed out, they were trying to enforce the leash law more, but "only in the Loop area." That means Anisq'Oyo Park, he added.

But Pecino agreed that relations needed to improve. He said that he was going to recommend that the special training that used to be given all officers assigned to the Foot Patrol be reinstituted, "probably by the end of the summer."

In response, an unidentified student commented that it's true that residents don't often see this side of the picture. "What we do see, however, is police breaking up parties, hitting people, dragging them away. We don't often see the 'garbage' you're referring to."

Several residents asked about the repeated instances of alleged unnecessary violence used by police recently and a year before over the 1988 Memorial Day weekend that resulted in several suspensions of officers and substantial civil settlements.

Brig Tratar, a third year student, stated that in an April 22, 1989 incident in front of the Foot Patrol office, he had been forced to lay face down in the street while an officer intentionally kicked him in the ribs. "But, because it was impossible to get the officer's badge number, I'm not able to file a complaint," he said.

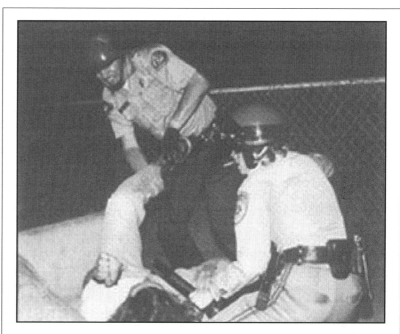

Police shown beating up an Isla Vista resident during the 1988 Memorial Day weekend melee in the 6600 block of Del Playa Drive, an area known as "The War Zone". Witnesses said two cops began swinging their nightclubs to break up a kegger with live music about 12:30. In response, people began throwing bottles at them. Two-dozen enforcements arrived around 1 AM by which time the crowd had grown to roughly 2,000 people. The situation quickly turned into a "police riot" as a phalanx of officers swept the street swinging nightclubs and yelling for people to go home. Several witnesses said the deputies entered apartments and trashed them. They then wrestled one guy to the pavement and threw him off the bluff and threw a pizza-delivery guy's car keys into the ocean. Eventually five officers were temporarily suspended and some I.V. residents received undisclosed cash awards from the County. Isla Vista *Free Press* photograph by Richard Reid.

Pecino responded that it is not necessary to have a badge number to file a complaint because it should be easy enough to get the name of the officer from the Sheriff Department's review that follows a complaint being filed. In response to a question by homeowner activist Leo Jacobson, however, Pecino admitted that this doesn't always work.

"What do you expect from officers who see other officers breaking the law?" asked Jacobson, recalling that some police behavior in I.V. has resulted in censure and suspensions.

Laura Price, president of the I.V. Park Board, appealed to both the audience and the police to understand that the police are victims of UCSB's over-enrollment policies just as much as I.V. residents.

"This is a community that has been turned into a pressure-cooker situation because of UCSB's overenrollment. . . Students are exploited by the University as well as by landlords. There's just too many people here and the rents are too high. In the long run, we're just going to have to say to the University to stop this over-enrollment. And the police should realize that they are being used as pawns in this policy."

"I'm not naive enough to expect officers to inform on other officers," Pecino replied. While they are instructed to report the use of excessive violence used by fellow officers, he said, "it's really tough" to expect that to happen. "We have to rely on supervising officers to see it, not fellow officers."

A poster that appeared throughout Isla Vista in the days following the 1988 Memorial Day police riot. Isla Vista *Free Press* photo.

Pecino assured everyone that he was beginning an examination of the April 22nd incident that resulted in several residents being hit with nightsticks and two persons being arrested, one of whom had the film in his camera exposed while in custody.

Laura Price, president of the I.V. Park Board, appealed to both the audience and the police to understand that the police are victims of UCSB's over-enrollment policies just as much as I.V. residents.

"This is a community that has been turned into a pressure-cooker situation because of UCSB's over-enrollment," she said emotionally. "Students are exploited by the University as well as by landlords. There's just too many people here and the rents are too high. In the long run, we're just going to have to say to the University to stop this over-enrollment. And the police should realize that they are being used as pawns in this policy."

Sgt. Olguin added that Isla Vista is a lot different place than when he served here eight years ago. "We never had any problems shutting down parties on Del Playa. But now, with the live bands, five-to-six hundred people — I'm not going in there. I might just be starting something I can't finish. The Fire Department won't respond anymore to fires in the dumpsters, because their trucks have been damaged by the crowds. And even paramedic trucks hesitate to go onto Del Playa on the weekends, unless we assure them we will break up any crowd."

"Plus, look at the statistics from last year," added Pecino. "Violent crimes are up in I.V., in all the categories people are concerned about."

Pecino made the point that the Foot Patrol was going to continue to enforce the ban on open containers of alcohol on the street, which was established two years previously. "This is a moral question to me," he said. "There is just too much alcohol abuse among young people — too many crazy people, especially highschoolers, along Del Playa. We're going to continue to try to control it."

UCSB Dean of Students Leslie Lawson (left) and UCSB Police Chief John MacPherson (right) at the May 4, 1989 meeting with residents. Isla Vista *Free Press* photograph.

Leslie Lawson, Dean of Students at UCSB, stated that the relationship between alcohol abuse and sexual abuse "shouldn't be underestimated."

Olguin also pointed out that there is too much work for the Foot Patrol. "We aren't a pro-active police force — we're just reactive, especially on weekends. Somebody calls us that several car windows have been smashed, but we don't have the time to respond because we're having to shut down loud parties."

Mitch Stockton, elected in November 1988 to the I.V. Park Board, lamented what he felt was the real problem. "We have no real say as a community over what the police do," he said. "This just builds frustration because no matter what the community says, it doesn't lead to any changes." Stockton was a leader in the 1983-84 campaign to establish a City of Isla Vista. "We need some authority over police in order to direct law enforcement priorities."

Boyd and a couple of other residents pointed out that if the Foot Patrol was going to start any new initiatives involving enforcing laws that have been largely ignored for years, there should be some attempt to warn the community.

Hewson also complained that the mounted officers controlling crowds during the recent Rugby

Weekend were "truly intimidating" and reminded her of a police state.

Pecino responded that they had received ten times as many compliments about the horses than complaints, and that they would continue their use because, "We'd rather have people complain about horses than riots."

Nothing concrete came out of the meeting except Pecino's pledge to re-establish special training programs for new Foot Patrol officers.

It's safe to assume, however, that the resumption of such training will have minimal impact on weekend policing activities when the Sheriff deploys an additional 20-30 officers into Isla Vista. These

Another Saturday night bust. Isla Vista *Free Press* photograph.

reinforcements are often from other police forces around the county; some are even volunteer reservists.

The *Free Press* has learned that Bill Wallace will be meeting with police officials this week in order to review the current situation.

"I'm still not receiving any complaints from I.V. residents about the police," Wallace said this week. "Maybe that just means that I'm out of the loop."

Note: Almost two decades have passed since this discussion among Isla Vista residents and the policing authorities. Has anything really changed? C.L.

CHAPTER 14

THE LEGACY OF STUDENT ACTIVISTS OF THE EIGHTIES

Each spring during its three years of publication (1987-89), the Isla Vista *Free Press* interviewed the student its editor felt had been most involved both on the UCSB campus and in Isla Vista. These interviews by Carmen Lodise have left an important legacy to students who want to get involved on campus and in Isla Vista.

Rich Laine

Rich Laine graduated from UCSB in 1987. Over five years, he had a broad range of involvement in student and community government. From a resident assistant in the dorms, to a year with Student Lobby and a term on the Isla Vista Community Council during the 1983-84 cityhood campaign; from a year on the Associated Student Legislative Council, to a year as A. S. vice president during a term the reigning president was forced out of office and the Chancellor was under siege; from a run at the A.S. presidency himself, only to step down at the last minute in solidarity with a (winning) candidate who was running almost solely on a platform of forcing Chancellor Robert Huttenback to resign (he did); to most of a year spent as a special consultant to A.S. Leg. Council when they took back control over operation of the UCen from the UCSB Administration. Rich Laine saw it all.

Rich Laine. Isla Vista Community Council (1983-84) and A. S. vice president (1984-85). Isla Vista *Free Press* photo.

Free Press: What started your involvement at UCSB? Were you active in high school and then you started right off here?

Laine: Actually no. Nothing to speak of in high school, and nothing much in my freshman year at UCSB. But early in my sophomore year a friend talked me into running in a special election for a vacancy on [the UCSB Associated Students] Leg. Council representing the dorms. I won, and got heavily involved in committee work and found that I had an interest and a facility to get things done.

During my junior year I had a part-time job as Metro Lobby (Student Lobby's local government activist) and was an RA in the dorms. It was in April 1985 that I ran for external vice president and won on a slate that included Jim Hickman as president and Todd Smith as the other (internal) vice president.

I was offended by the Administration's machinations about I.V. cityhood (in 1984) at the UC Regents. It was all so unethical. The Administration was telling them in a sense that I.V. was the University's own little fiefdom to do with it what they want.

RICH LAINE

We started out so optimistically. Each of us had good working relations with the Administration and quite a bit of experience in A.S. But it all turned into a nightmare with the revelations that Jim had been involved the year before in some questionable expenditures of a few thousand dollars of A.S. funds, which was compounded by some inadequate financial oversight by the then-executive director. The result was a big loss of credibility as Jim was forced to resign, a $100,000 deficit for the year we were working in, and a hold placed on all of our platform ideas.

At the time, I was disappointed as to how little help and support we got from [UCSB Vice Chancellor] Ed Birch and the rest of the administration. They said as much, "It's A.S.'s problem, let A.S. clean it up."

In retrospect I learned a lot from the situation about how bureaucratic structures work, and A.S.'s accountability system was strengthened considerably.

Free Press: Why did you run for A.S. president in the spring of 1986, and more importantly, why did you drop out in favor of Doug Yates?

Laine: Based on that year's experience, I felt that A.S. needed a president who had hands-on knowledge of the roll it plays in the governance of UCSB, plus a person who had a working relationship with the players, especially given [Chancellor Robert] Huttenback's possible resignation.

By March, Todd, myself and Ken Greenstein [who had replaced Hickman] were convinced that Huttenback should resign, but we talked ourselves into waiting until April before we confronted him with it. In his office, we asked him flat out to resign. We told him the biggest student issues were:

#1. Over-enrollment

#2. His unwillingness to keep his word

Several times he had kept his word with us only as long as it was convenient for him. We felt the University couldn't operate like this. He, of course, laughed off our recommendation.

We had acted on our own, relating what we felt was in the best interests of students. But, on the way out of his office, we noticed that there was a committee of faculty waiting to see him. It turned out that this was the famous meeting in which they asked him to resign.

Shortly after that, I concluded that Huttenback would resign, the only question was when. I felt that dropping out of the race for (A.S.) president while throwing my support to Yates was the quickest way to accomplish this.

Free Press: What are the major issues in campus/community relations in your opinion?

Free Press: What are the major issues in campus/community relations in your opinion?

Laine: Over-enrollment, unquestionably. [Then-Chancellor Robert] Huttenback felt that the University was an island unto itself, and that he didn't have to cooperate with any of the surrounding communities.

RICH LAINE

Laine: Over-enrollment, unquestionably. Huttenback felt that the University was an island unto itself, and that he didn't have to cooperate with any of the surrounding communities. But, Huttenback wasn't the only one! There are too many old bones around here and before things will change, they're going to have to shift some people out. They need some new personalities.

Huttenback was a bad leader with some possibly bad followers, and it's possible that he corrupted the rest of his leadership.

Free Press: Is Isla Vista a community?

Laine: In a sense. It certainly has a personality of its own. Unfortunately, it's rapidly becoming a slum and students don't see the access ways to improve it.

Free Press: What about Isla Vista cityhood? I know you started out quite skeptical about it.

Laine: I'd like to think it is the best way. Self-government would help and it would give the community a better bargaining position with the University. Because even with a city, there still would be need to be a lot of cooperation and negotiating with the U.

I was offended by the Administration's machinations about I.V. cityhood [in 1984] at the UC Regents. It was all so unethical. The Administration was telling them in a sense that I.V. was the University's own little fiefdom, to do with it what they want.

The Regents don't really know what's going on in Isla Vista. Gardner might, or at least he knows what the chancellor says. But none of them really know. And I think it is a shame because it's impossible to separate I.V. from UCSB — there are just too many links.

Ken Greenstein

Ken Greenstein began UCSB in the fall of 1982. After a year in Francisco Torres Residence Hall,

he lived in Isla Vista until graduation, except for six months he spent as an intern in Washington, D.C. Ken was elected to the A.S. Legislative Council in the spring of 1985 and was appointed A.S. President after the elected president was forced to resign. He also spent a year active in peace issues and in A.S. Student Lobby, where he was part of the effort to rid the faculty of it association with the CIA.

Free Press: Were you involved in student government and politics in high school?

Greenstein: I was just a jock. I played basketball at Beverly Hills High. I was totally non-political, I played a lot of cards, and me and my friends did a lot of stupid things.

Free Press: What started your involvement at UCSB?

Greenstein: I helped found a fraternity, ZBT. I had rushed an existing one but didn't make it. So I got mad and helped get the new one going. I thought

Ken Greenstein. Associated Students president (1985-86). Isla Vista *Free Press* photograph.

frats were important — a lot of my friends joined, the social life, the co-operative living. I was a vice president and got a lot of projects and committees going and that was fun. But as I become more politically involved, I found that my values were conflicting with those of other members. There was a lot of prejudice and conscious elitism. After two years, I dropped out.

Free Press: You said as you became "politically involved"?

Greenstein: During the 1984 [U.S. presidential] election, I began researching the issues a lot. I guess I had always suspected that there was something gravely wrong with our foreign and domestic policies. Some of my classes opened my eyes. But I guess it was Stockwell's speeches about the CIA and becoming friends with a lot of progressive people that really turned by around. I was involved with the Die-In in Storke Plaza in early 1985, some other peace things, and then ran for A.S. in April.

Free Press: What did you learn from your experience in student government?

Greenstein: That I hate bureaucracies! Also, how powerless students are without direct action. Students — in numbers — need to confront the Administration (or the local government or whatever) to actually have success. You can only make small changes through negotiations; they have the staff, the time, the information that students (and residents) don't have. We can only get something accomplished with the threat of confrontation. So we have to inspire people that their empowerment will actually lead to impacts that will improve their lives.

Free Press: Is Isla Vista a community?

Greenstein: I sure think it is. I really missed it – especially the Food Co-op – while I was in D.C. last year (on an internship). But because of the high turnover of residents, a lot of people take too much for granted here and they don't make much effort to improve the community. But I.V. has shown that when there is a threat, a lot of people unite, which has produced a lot of good community organizations and projects.

KEN GREENSTEIN

Free Press: Is Isla Vista a community?

Greenstein: I sure think it is. I really missed it – especially the Food Co-op – while I was in D.C. last year (on an internship). But because of the high turnover of residents, a lot of people take too much for granted here and they don't make much effort to improve the community. But I.V. has shown that when there is a threat, a lot of people unite, which has produced a lot of good community organizations and projects.

Free Press: What do you think of Isla Vista Cityhood?

Greenstein: We definitely need it in order to improve the services, for rent control, and to end the dominance of special interests. With I.V. cityhood, people would realize that participating in community is really the right place to be.

With the demise of the Isla Vista Community Council, maybe the Associated Students should get more involved in I.V. We can't leave it for the Federation and special interests.

Javier LaFianza

Javier LaFianza was a fifth-year senior when the Free Press *interviewed him in Isla Vista in May 1989. Over several years, LaFianza was involved with the re-assertion of student-control over the UCen, a police/student relations committee, and the Student Fee Advisory Committee before being elected A.S. President for 1988-89.*

He also served a year term on the Isla Vista Community Council, 1986-87, and was involved with the hunger strike on campus during 1989, which was attempting to secure a two-course ethnic studies requirement.

Free Press: What did you learn from your experience in student government?

LaFianza: Before I became A.S. President, I had believed that you could get things done by working through the process channels that were provided. Even though I'd been stalled in the process for years before then, I felt that becoming president would help — the increased stature would overcome this. What I discovered is that you have to resort to pressure tactics to get things done because the bureaucracy and the Chancellor respond a lot better when there is some sense of urgency. Some combination of process and other empowering methods works best.

There is a definite undercurrent of hostility (in Isla Vista) coming from the police and a complete lack of respect toward residents, and this is a recurring problem over the years. This is a high-stress, overcrowded environment to deal with – both for residents and the police. And it's all caused by over-enrollment . . .

JAVIER LAFIANZA

I learned, too, that you can't make everybody happy — you have to find your own issues and stick to those, and push all the way.

Free Press: What do you feel was accomplished over the past year?

Javier LaFianza. Isla Vista Community Council (1986-87) and Associated Students president (1988-89). Isla Vista *Free Press* photograph.

LaFianza: Our biggest accomplishments were in the field of ethnic diversity. The faculty vote on the ethnic studies requirement won't be known for a few more days [it eventually came in in favor of a one-course requirement], but the entire campus community is a whole lot more aware of the issue how.

Plus the $7,500 A.S. put up for the multi-cultural center has resulted in the funding of a $45,000 program including adding an Asian EOP counselor. In fact, I heard David Hough of the Student Fee Advisory Committee say recently that 80-90% of the money they spent this year was on diversity issues and this would not have happened without the climate we created.

Also, we had minimum student representation added to Faculty Committees, and they will be considering making these voting members at the next Faculty Senate meeting [they remained advisory]. All in all, I think it was a very good year — a productive year. We did more educating than perhaps in any other recent year.

Free Press: What is your opinion of the new chancellor (Barbara Uehling) and her style of leadership, which I've heard is to push various segments of the campus community into making decisions without necessarily stating her position on the issues?

LaFianza: I think in fact the Administration is paralyzed, and I hear a lot of concern from the faculty about this, too. They never gave an adequate response to the activism on ethnic issues. I wonder if Uehling is all that aware of what's going on? We had to explain to her one time what a CSO was! She trusts too much in the conduits of information to her, and if these are polluted or clueless, she gets incomplete and tainted information. The result is she appears to be uninvolved.

Free Press: What are the major campus/community issues now?

LaFianza: Obviously what's going on with the police is a major issue. When cops start enforcing the leash law (for dogs) in the middle of a festival at a park in I.V., something is definitely wrong. Certainly, communication between police and residents is lacking and needs to be dealt with, but the leash law enforcement means that there is something else going on. There is a definite undercurrent of hostility coming from the police and complete lack of respect toward residents, and this is a recurring problem over the years.

> *I.V. needs community self-determination to deal with [the problems caused by over-enrollment], yet this is exactly what the University [Administration] won't allow. Maybe they will figure out that this needs to happen now that all of these problems are consistently happening.*
>
> JAVIER LAFIANZA

This is a high-stress, over-crowded environment to deal with — both for residents and the police. And we need more than band-aid solutions.

And it's all caused by over-enrollment — what you might say is the second problem, but the first problem is caused by the second. It's so obvious — there are too many cars, bike accidents, the problem with police . . . .

I.V. needs community self-determination to deal with this, yet this is exactly what the University [Administration] won't allow. Maybe they will figure out that this needs to happen now that all of these problems are consistently happening. The proposed redevelopment agency is a case in point. What will be the governance board? Appointments from various groups (like Wallace wants) is okay for some of them, but the majority should be elected. And Wallace is noted for not appointing students and I.V. residents to County advisory boards. Also trash and recycling is a problem in Isla Vista, and one that should be easy to solve.

CHAPTER 15

THE ISLA VISTA TREE: GONE BUT NOT FORGOTTEN

On January 28, 1983, the tree that had come to be the symbol of Isla Vista's dreams of self-governance, fell off the cliff into the ocean, the victim of a particularly severe winter storm.

News of the event spread quickly through the community. The next morning, a flood of memories rushed through me as I gazed at the empty spot at the edge of the bluff in the County's Del Playa Park where the tree had tenaciously clung for so many years.

What had the Isla Vista Tree meant in this town? The elegant cypress had come to represent Isla Vista's quest for self-governance as an offshoot of the community-building efforts in the 1970s and '80s. A drawing

The Isla Vista Tree, the symbol of Isla Vista self-governance, fell into the ocean on January 28, 1983. Photograph by Doug Martin for the Isla Vista *Free Press*.

The Isla Vista Tree, along with the title from Carl Sandburg's 1936 poem "The People, Yes", is pictured on the many thousands of bright yellow and red-orange buttons that have been distributed through the years. The button symbolizes Isla Vista's quest for self-governance.

of the tree had been used as a logo on the letterhead of the Isla Vista Community Council (IVCC), which is now inactive, and it remains the letterhead of the Isla Vista Recreation and Park District — certainly the central institutional embodiment of that movement.

A drawing of the tree also is the centerpiece of the several

Isla Vista Community Council representative Sharleen Weed touching up the Welcome to Isla Vista sign that stood on Los Carneros Road during most of the 1980s and '90s. Isla Vista *Free Press* photograph.

generations of the Welcome to Isla Vista signs on Los Carneros Road. In addition, several thousand yellow and red buttons proclaiming "Isla Vista: the People, Yes" as a border around the tree have been distributed over the years. The phrase was adopted from Carl Sandburg's famous poem, which is excerpted in the Afterward, entitled "The People, Yes."

Stationary letterhead of the Isla Vista Recreation & Park District. Drawing by Al Plyley.

And, a 1980 Park District poster calling attention to the growth of community institutions in the decade following the razing of the Bank of America during the 1970 civil disturbances here, pictures the I.V. Tree growing out of the ashes of the Bank.

It is that poster that was adapted for the cover of the website on which this book is based: www.islavistahistory.com

As I remember it, Eric Hutchens and Al Plyley were the two individuals who did the most to popularize the tree as a symbol of I.V.'s community-building movement. But, it was so immediately a hit that there was a big stink made when some politicians tried to use it as a logo in their campaigns.

It's ironic that the tree grew in the only County-owned park in Isla Vista at the time (the next 26-plus acres of parks in I.V. were purchased and developed by the community through the I.V. Park District). The alienation between the community and County government was painfully obvious when the IVCC asked the County Parks Department to replace the tree with a new one and to create a plaque memorializing the tree near the spot it once grew. Of course, the IVCC asked that the plaque include a picture of the tree and the statement "Isla Vista: The People, Yes." The director of the County Parks Department at the time, Mike Pahos, adamantly refused to do this, stating that this slogan was, to him, advocacy of Isla Vista cityhood.

After an appeal to the County Parks Commission, and much discussion of the difference between community-building and one particular local government option for Isla Vista — and only after the cameras from the local TV station arrived in the meeting and the Isla Vista delegation threatened to read the entire 140-some pages of Sandburg's poem — did the Parks Commission agree to recommend to the Board of Supervisors that the plaque be installed with the wording requested for a total cost of

$400.

Isla Vista resident Jeannie Hodges cast the plaque in her studio on campus. She requested the $400 to pay only for the materials used.

The County Parks Department installed the rock with the plaque in what is now called Ocean View Park on May 17, 1984

Shortly thereafter, a rugby team from Santa Barbara, in a drunken stupor,

The plaque showing The People, Yes button, which commemorates the Isla Vista Tree, was designed and cast by I.V. resident Jeannie Hodges. The plaque was reluctantly installed by the County of Santa Barbara in 1984 in the one park the County owned at that time – the setting in which the tree had become famous. Isla Vista *Free Press* photograph.

pushed the rock off the bluff onto the beach twenty-five feet below. It took a giant crane to restore the rock and plaque to the spot it can be seen in today. And, the rock has been more adequately secured to the ground.

So, while the Isla Vista Tree is gone, it is not forgotten.

And, the tree did outlast the Bank of America's re-built bank in Isla Vista. That must mean something.

CHAPTER 16

THE ISLA VISTA ADVENTURE

Before I moved to Isla Vista, I had never lived anyplace more than three years in a row. Yet, I lived in Isla Vista for the better part of two decades (1972 to 1992) and a few more years after that. It's not that I didn't ask myself why now and then.

After all, Isla Vista is crowded and noisy. People litter its streets like they don't really care and rents are out-of-sight for what you get. And the powers-that-be (the UCSB Administration, the County of Santa Barbara, and absentee landlords) don't give a damn about its residents' quality of life.

The reason I stayed so long is that Isla Vista is in many ways quite an extraordinary town. First, you get to meet so many fascinating people — most of who come to I.V. because of the University. Secondly, I like getting on my bike, riding down the street and running into my friends — just like in a small town anywhere.

Thirdly, it's unruly. Most I.V. residents are living on their own for the first time and often push the limits of what's acceptable. Combine this with the "occupying force" attitude of the police, the reactionary posturing of the UCSB Administration, and the inappropriateness of County government, which is designed to govern rural not urban areas, and you have a very special situation — I.V. has always felt like liberated territory and I hope it always will.

Unruly: A 1989 protest on the UCSB campus. There is a cycle to student demonstrations: There are almost none in the fall, a few between Christmas and the Easter break, then one almost daily in May. Isla Vista *Free Press* photo.

But what I liked most about Isla Vista back then was that it was so easy to get involved in community-building, and how rewarding it was. When I moved to I.V. I discovered that all you had to do was talk your friends into doing something that made sense and then put in a lot of hard work implementing it. Plus, all the discussions were at the right level — we were thinking globally and acting locally long before John and Yoko popularized the phrase. It was the perfect cure for my severe case of alienation, brought on by the studied realization that the so-called Land of the Free had become a racist, sexist, militaristic nation. I rolled up my sleeves and went to work.

The vision of the community as a laboratory was a good guide as long as we were working in the vacuum the County and University created — the total absence of a community infrastructure. Following the tumultuous period of 1968-70, there was a lot of cooperation between the County, UCSB, and I.V.'s community activists. But the planning and organizing began to create a momentum of its own, and when I.V.'s residents decided that independent cityhood was the logical next step in community development, it led us back into conflict with the local power structure.

The UCSB Administration and the County were thrown off balance by the events of 1970 as the whole world discovered the ghetto they had consciously cooperated to build. For a few years, these forces of reaction were willing to throw us some money to run a few programs in order to keep us busy, but they weren't about to let us get out from under their control.

The creation of these support organizations did make Isla Vista a better place in which to live, and the Park District and CETA jobs sustained the community-building spirit well into the 1980s. However, by the mid-1980s – just 15 years after the events of 1970 and the conclusions of the Trow Report — both the County and the University put down the other foot, forcefully reminding everyone involved that Isla Vista was a company town, and as far as they were concerned, always would be.

> *. . . the local (UCSB) Administration's attitude that the improvement of Isla Vista's environment was of secondary importance in the long-range development of the campus . . . reflects a failure to consider the campus and Isla Vista as an integrated University community. . . .*
>
> THE TROW REPORT

As Isla Vista went through the 1990s, with dramatically reduced financial resources, the community lost the original goal in which each organization worked to empower its constituents, so that in a networking of constituencies, they could empower the whole town. Community agencies now, for the most part, just provide good services.

And whereas I.V. was once the area's fountainhead of innovative community programs of recycling, growth-control, cottage industries, auto-reduction, pesticide-free parks, etc., this beacon pretty much fell silent a few years ago.

The battle to save Perfect Park (1989-91) was the last major community campaign in defense of the town's honor and it was an internal fight provoked by an ex-resident of Isla Vista, County Supervisor Bill Wallace, in a cynical move to pit the town's activists against the local fundamentalist church that owned the property and planned to put a 2-1/2 story building on it.

It was the failure to achieve cityhood that caused the town to lose the momentum created in the 1970s. Advisory-level government can be sustained for only so long!

First, Isla Vista needed cityhood to get access to the resources required to implement the many projects set forth by its youthful planners. If the town had become a city in the 1970s, City Hall would be in the building where the Cantina Restaurant is now and the Medical Clinic expansion of the late '80s would instead have been to incorporate it into the town's community center. Instead, Isla Vistans still have to go to the County and to UCSB to ask for the scraps off their plates. And if the people making the requests are elected leaders, their requests are discounted in favor of the recommendations of a tiny minority of cranky homeowners.

Secondly, Isla Vistans needed cityhood in order to be treated as equals in the give-and-take required for a healthy relationship with UCSB. As it is, Isla Vista has to adjust to whatever enrollment level the University declares, no matter how outrageous.

Thirdly, if Isla Vista had obtained cityhood in the 1970s, the city would have purchased Perfect Park before the St. Athanasius Church did and Wallace wouldn't have been able to do his mischief. Instead, Isla Vista remains a fiefdom, pushed around by the same cabal that created it.

In a sense, UCSB is the most powerful 'citizen' in Isla Vista, yet in our opinion it has refused to assume its proportionate civic responsibility.

THE TROW REPORT

One concept of how to better mesh auto and bicycle traffic in Isla Vista's downtown area. This idea would one-way Embarcadero del Mar running toward the ocean with traffic returning toward El Colegio on Embarcadero del Norte. It's safe to say that the town would have a lot more of these kind of physical improvements if Isla Vista had become a city back in the 1970s or 1980s. One of nearly 50 drawings by Byron Holmes, Jr. in the 120-page document <u>Recommendations for Isla Vista Planning</u> (1973) from the Isla Vista Community Council.

Finally, Isla Vistans needed cityhood to show ourselves what we know innately — that self-government produces collective responsibility. Instead, the police treat townies without respect and residents feel little urgency to conform to rules they don't make.

What does it mean that the County and University don't trust a coalition between the brightest 18 to 24-year-olds the State has to offer and a long tradition of caring community activists to govern the town they live in — especially when the County/University/landlord alliance has repeatedly demonstrated its incompetence to do it right? This is a mind-boggling indictment of the American educational system and governance traditions. It's no wonder less than half of U.S. citizens register to vote and only half of those who do register bother to show up at the polls.

About 1990, Wallace justified an appointed (rather than elected) project advisory committee (PAC) to the then-forming Isla Vista Redevelopment Agency by saying: "If you have elections in Isla Vista, you get the kind of people you have at the Park District." This is after he used to be an elected official in Isla Vista himself (1971-73), used his popularity in I.V. to get elected to the Goleta Water Board in 1976, and relied on Isla Vista voters to keep him on the board of supervisors for 20 years.

And it's the County-appointed PAC, heavily favoring propertied interests, that has brought the town the so-called Isla Vista Master Plan of 2007 that favors cars over pedestrians and bicyclists and will lead to more overcrowding in a place that's already the most densely packed town within hundreds of miles.

Needless to say, a Master Plan created by elected Isla Vistans would look a lot different.

Was Wallace right? Is there something inherently wrong with elected leadership in Isla Vista? While I have often disagreed with specific decisions of people elected to

The LAFCO Sign. Left to right: Harley Augustino, Carmen Lodise, and Logan Green. For years, this wooden relic resided at the home of the informal leader of Isla Vista's quest for self-governance. In 1992, Lodise passed it on to Mitch Stockton with much ritualistic ceremony. Stockton later passed it on to Pegeen Souter where it stood near her family's hot tub. The sign was passed on from Harley to Logan at Lodise's retirement party in December 2004. The sign was originally "lifted" from its spot outside the board of supervisors' hearing room in Santa Barbara during a LAFCO meeting by IVCC Representative Cindy Wachter and Lodise one afternoon in 1976 -- with the assistance of County Supervisor Frank Frost. LAFCO three times vetoed holding an election on establishing a City of Isla Vista. Photograph by Sally Derevan.

the Isla Vista Park Board, through the years they have been some of the most caring and thoughtful persons I have ever met. It is the Park District that gave land to the Southeast Asian refugees for their gardens in the 1970s, that gave shelter and support to I.V.'s homeless through the years, and that allocates crucial assistance to the town's youth-serving agencies — while tending a steadily expanding and improving park system (where almost none had been provided by the County).

And it's the Park District that keeps the live music playing in the center of town.

What's more, the Park Board listens to their opposition, usually affording them a lot more courtesy and respect than is returned.

What Isla Vista needs is more democracy, not less. But this will be difficult to achieve unless there is another great conflagration or unless its leadership can figure out how to grab the magic ring — the transformation of Isla Vista into city.

Because of the unique local environment of Isla Vista, the ingredients are present for a promising experiment in community development.

THE TROW REPORT

When will the County and the University finally realize that Isla Vista self-government is in their best interests, too?

And what's with Bill Wallace? How could a man whose political career depended so much on his support from Isla Vista voters, wind up showing the town the shaft so many times? After all, he failed to get the votes for the Camino Pescadero Mall, for continued funding of the IVCC, and for a citizen vote on Isla Vista cityhood. He was a decade late raising the over-enrollment issue and he tried to give away Perfect Park to a right-wing church.

However, in the interest of full-disclosure, I have to admit I voted for him every time he was on the ballot and my newspaper endorsed him for supervisor in 1988 over a pro-cityhood and rent control candidate. My endorsement headline read: "Wallace, Warts and All." Why would I do this?

Well, it's complicated. First was his integrity on the biggest issue of all, which is Isla Vista cityhood. Wallace always ran openly on a platform supporting a combined city of Isla Vista and Goleta, even though he knew that most Isla Vistans (and Goletans) opposed that option. His aim seemed to be to spread Isla Vista's block vote on environmental issues over as many acres of Goleta as possible. The irony here is that, while most outsiders didn't trust Isla Vistans to run a city government, Wallace didn't trust Goleta voters to run a city without the hammer of Isla Vista's liberal vote. But he openly ran on that position, so he couldn't be faulted.

Secondly, he was right on all the other countywide issues, he worked the hardest of any supervisor to know the issues, and he was smarter than most of the rest of them combined.

And then there was his opposition. Except for 1988, all of his opponents were either dullards or in cahoots with the developers. So, supporting him was the obvious thing to do, although Isla Vista certainly has paid a price.

However, it's pretty clear that it's the revolving door of UCSB officials, not Wallace, that is at fault for the continued drift of Isla Vista — and that's the way they want it. It is also obvious that, more than anyone else, Wallace had the chance to challenge that, but he decided to play it another way. To him, Isla Vista simply provided the shock troops while he held his thumb in the dike of urbanization for two decades. Maybe he just wasn't up to the fight to shake up the master/servant relationships of a company town.

Even though Isla Vistans have been denied a greater destiny so far, Isla Vista is still a town where most of its residents care more about ideals than money and whose residents would like to give more to their community if afforded the opportunity.

THE PEOPLE, YES

by Carl Sandburg

It's unclear to me how and why the title of this 1936 poem became associated with the Isla Vista community building efforts following the civil disturbances of 1969-70. I think Eric Hutchens had a lot to do with it and the artist Al Plyley did the most to popularize it. What follows are my excerpts from a poem that runs over 140 pages. – C.L.

The people is Everyman, everybody.
Everybody is you and me and all others.
What everybody says is what we all say.
And what is it we all say?
The people say and unsay,
    put up and tear down
    and put together again
a builder, wrecker, and builder again
This is the people.

In the people is the eternal child,
the wandering gypsy, the pioneer homeseeker,
    the singer of home sweet home.

From the people the countries get their armies.
The long wars and the short wars will come on
    the air.
How many got killed and how the war ended
And who got what and the price paid
And how there were tombs for the unknown
    Soldier,
The boy nobody knows the name of,
The boy whose great fame is that of the masses,
The millions of names too many to write on a
    tomb,
The heroes, the cannon fodder, the living targets,
The mutilated and sacred dead,
The people, yes.
And after the strife of war begins the strife of
    peace.

What the people learn out of lifting and hauling
and waiting and losing and laughing
Goes into a scroll, an almanac, a record folding
and unfolding, and the music goes down and
    around:

The story goes on and on, happens, forgets to
    happen,
goes out and meets itself coming in,
puts on disguises and drops them.

The people laugh, yes, the people laugh.
They have to in order to live and survive under
lying politicians, lying labor skates,
lying racketeers of business, lying newspapers,
    lying ads.
The people laugh even at lies that cost them toil
    and bloody exactions.

For a long time the people may laugh,
until a day comes when the laughter changes key
    and tone
has something it didn't have.
Then there is a scurrying
and a noise of discussion
and an asking of the question what is it the people
    want.
Then there is a pretense of giving the people what
    they want,
with jokers, trick clauses, delays and
    continuances,
with lawyers and fixers, playboys and
    ventriloquists,
big time promises.

Time goes by and the gains are small for the years
    go slow,
yet the gains can be counted
and the laughter of the people foretokening revolt
carries fear to those who wonder how far it will
    go
and where to block it.

APPENDIX A: THE TROW REPORT:
UCSB'S RESPONSIBILITIES TO ISLA VISTA

*Note: This is a more detailed examination of the Trow Report than appeared in Chapter 3. --
C.L.*

In April 1970, the UC Regents established a seven-person committee called The Commission on Isla Vista to "make recommendations for eliminating or ameliorating the causes of unrest in Isla Vista." The committee, which included UC Berkeley sociologist Martin Trow (after who the final report was popularly named) and Ira M. Heyman (former Professor of City & Regional Planning at UC Berkeley and Chancellor there from 1980 to 1990), chose "to make practical recommendations about the University's role in Isla Vista... [which were] designed to change the character of Isla Vista in ways that will reduce its potential for violence and destruction, and strengthen its potential as . . . a vital community." The Commission made its final report to the UC Regents in October of that year.

The Trow Report's observations and recommendations remain a standard by which the University's actions and policies toward Isla Vista can be judged.

What follows are some selected excerpts from the Report's Preface and 100 pages of Observations and Recommendations, which are reproduced here in bold print, as are several of the recommendations from the report.

I have also included COMMENTS as to what, to my knowledge, has been accomplished (and what has not) since the Trow Report was published. This analysis first appeared in the Isla Vista Free Press on March 30, 1987 and has been partially updated for the publication of this book (2008).

Note: On July 16, 2008 I wrote UCSB Chancellor Henry T. Yang requesting assistance in updating the Trow Report for the publication of this book. My letter, which was copied to several UC Regents, read in part:

"I am requesting that you and/or your staff review and comment on the section of my website history of Isla Vista regarding the Trow Report, a report – requested by the UC Regents — by several UC scholars on the causes of the 1970 civil disturbances in Isla Vista. I did such a review in 1987 based on interviews with and public statements of UCSB Administration officials. However, that was over 20 years ago.

"In addition, I am aware of many positive changes in campus/community relations during your years as chancellor. Thus, I think it would be unnecessarily antagonistic and even less than truthful to let the record stand as of 1987. However, I do not personally feel close enough to the community these days to write such an update myself, and therefore have asked for your assistance."

On August 11, 2008, I received the following polite email response from the chancellor:

From: **Henry Yang** (henry.yang@chancellor.ucsb.edu)
Sent: Mon 8/11/08 3:49 PM
To: Carmen Lodise (lodise0711@hotmail.com)
Cc: Cecile Cuttitta (Cecile.cuttitta@ucop.edu)

Dear Mr. Lodise,

I write in response to your letter of July 16, 2008, regarding your website on the history of Isla Vista.

This is quite a project you have proposed and we wish you the very best with converting your website into a book. There are a number of sites that may contain information of the type you are seeking on the main UCSB website. These include the Isla Vista Commission home page (http://senate.ucsb.edu/ivcommission) and the UCSB Long Range Development Plan site (http://www.ucsbvision2025.com).

As you may know, I formed the Isla Vista Commission in June 2005, in response to the recommendations of another committee, the Isla Vista Action Group. The IV Commission coordinates the many ongoing activities that are currently part of the Isla Vista-UCSB relationship, and initiates or assists in the development of new programs intended to serve the mutual interests of I.V. and our campus. Since its inception, programs such as IV Live, the Magic Lantern film series, and IV Arts have been initiated. Our campus is dedicated to a cooperative effort among campus and community offices and constituencies to help make Isla Vista a safer place to learn, live, work, enjoy recreation and pursue safe public events.

I hope this information is helpful. Thank you for your interest in UC Santa Barbara and for taking the time to write. Again, best wishes with your book project.

Sincerely,

Henry T. Yang
Chancellor

The reader is welcome to review the suggested websites.

-- C.L.

SELECTED OBSERVATIONS from the Trow Report

If there is one thread running through all of our deliberations and recommendations, it is that the University can no longer ignore, if it ever could, the conditions under which the bulk of its students live and spend the greater part of their time while at the University. What goes on in Isla Vista is as central to the University's life and functions as what goes on in its laboratories and lecture rooms. page iii, Preface.

The University cannot act in Isla Vista just as it does on its own campus; but neither can it refuse to act there at all. That principle, to which we have been persuaded by everything we have learned in our inquiry, is present in all of our recommendations. page iii, Preface.

Isla Vista is deeply scarred by the events of the past year and its very survival as a place to house a university community is in jeopardy. It has been largely ignored in the past by both the University and the County government and consequently has not developed long-standing institutions. Without indigenous institutions, the community can continue to be torn apart. But if increasing numbers of Isla Vista residents can feel that they are able to improve their own environment, Isla Vista can become a distinguished university community. Because of the unique local environment of Isla Vista, the ingredients are present for a promising experiment in community development. page 3.

To the extent that UCSB has had a policy toward Isla Vista, it appears to have been to avoid extensive involvement in the affairs of the community. Until some official steps were taken recently to formulate a more aggressive policy, there was no statement of policy from the Chancellor specifying a philosophy of UCSB relationship to Isla Vista. page 55.

COMMENT: In anticipation of something like this comment in the Trow Report, a UCSB policy toward Isla Vista was hurriedly written over t he summer of 1970. However, it was little adhered to and soon forgotten, as the statement in 1987 of Vice-Chancellor of Student and Community Affairs Edward Birch demonstrated: "It's a mistake to think that there is one University policy toward the community, because there isn't the unanimity among the various parties here and we just don't have one, overall policy. [Isla Vista *Free Press* interview, March 30, 1987]

The general attitude of the University as perceived by the students, as well as by several members of the administration has been a hands-off doctrine summed up as: Isla Vista is not University campus; Isla Vista is Isla Vista and the University is the University. page 57.

COMMENT: Even several years later, it didn't appear that the UCSB Administration's attitude had changed much toward the community as the comments of two subsequent chancellors, Daniel Aldrich (1986-87) and Barbara Uehling (1988-94), indicate.

Daniel Aldrich: "Isla Vista is not University campus; Isla Vista is contiguous to the campus. As such, the campus has to interact positively and sensitively with any community so close. The campus has to be a good neighbor, has to work constructively with the community." [I.V. *Free Press* interview March 30, 1987]

Daniel Aldrich was the caretaker chancellor at UCSB between the firing of Robert Huttenback in 1986 and the hiring of Barbara Uehling in 1988. Aldrich had been the well-liked chancellor at UC Irvine and he was brought out of retirement for this short-term stint. A decent man, he and his wife could often be seen strolling on the beach and picking up trash. However, he just didn't get it when it came to Isla Vista.

Uehling: "The University has a special responsibility to our students who live in I.V. But exercising this responsibility is difficult because ... we have no legal jurisdiction there." [I.V. *Free Press* interview, February 15, 1989]

Although she had previously been the chancellor at both the University of Missouri and Oklahoma State University, she soon got run off by the UCSB faculty, who found her cold and uninvolved. Uehling never really tried to get to know Isla Vista and certainly gave no sign of having read the Trow Report.

A report to the Regents by the consulting firm of Pereira & Luckman in 1958 commented on Isla Vista's small lots narrow streets, lack of sidewalks and absence of street lights. Pereira & Luckman recommended that the University assist the county government in developing a "vital, well-balanced community, which will be most conducive to the University's healthy, long-term growth." It appears that no initiative was taken as a result of the recommendation. The County was not consulted for a joint land use plan for the area, and subsequent UCSB Long Range Plans in 1958, 1963, and 1968 basically ignored Isla Vista.

This was most striking in the 1963 and 1968 plans. By 1960 it was already apparent that students living off-campus would be seeking housing in Isla Vista, but this was not reflected in the 1963 plan. The University Planner in Berkeley reacted to this omission as follows:

"The seeming lack of concern for 'what goes on in Isla Vista' as evidenced by the Plan Study's lack of indication of land uses, circulation patterns, and current state of building development in this area, should be corrected at once. The campus obviously has a great stake in Isla Vista's growth coupled with and complementary to the campus itself for it is the campus' only residential neighbor. As at other campuses, intensive efforts must be made to coordinate physical planning of campus and community."

Again, alarming words went unheeded . . . . By 1968, the University almost completely surrounded Isla Vista, but the name "Isla Vista" appeared in passing only a few places in the 1968 UCSB Long-Range Development Plan. Perhaps symbolically, the maps included in that

Report used nine colors to illustrate features of the campus and a stern gray to color Isla Vista, the airport and other "non-university" areas. pages 57-8.

The Commission believes (that there has been) . . . an inability on the part of the UCSB administration to balance realistically and wisely its reluctance to intervene in affairs which affect the interests of private parties with the need to protect the orderly development of a University community in Isla Vista. page 66.

. . . the local (UCSB) administration's attitude that the improvement of Isla Vista's environment was of secondary importance in the long-range development of the campus . . . reflects a failure to consider the campus and Isla Vista as an integrated University community. page 67

In summary, in a situation that generates a great deal of misunderstanding and hostility, the University has made rather limited attempts to ameliorate tensions or improve living conditions. At the same time, the University continues to expand its enrollment [then 13,733, 19,082 in 1989, and 25,000 in the 2010 LRDP currently under review: CL] without providing additional attractive living quarters on campus. In a sense, UCSB is the most powerful 'citizen' in Isla Vista, yet in our opinion it has refused to assume its proportionate civic responsibility. page 76.

SELECTIVE RECOMMENDATIONS (pages 85-100)

#1A. That UCSB adopt and take immediate steps to implement policies recognizing that Isla Vista is an integral part of the University community and that UCSB's vital interests are involved in improving the quality of life there.

Rationale: UCSB has a vital interest in Isla Vista; its campuses virtually surround the area; approximately two-thirds of its student body lives in Isla Vista; . . . the functioning of UCSB as an educational institution is greatly affected by events occurring in Isla Vista.

The Commission believes that the unique relationship of UCSB and Isla Vista requires a higher degree of University involvement in local affairs . . . . (UCSB) has not enunciated and carried out an aggressive policy for dealing with the problems of Isla Vista. It has failed to intervene effectively in the pattern of Isla Vista land development, thereby allowing the conditions to arise in which dissatisfaction and frustration could flourish.

Recent events indicate the need for leadership to aid in the creation of a substructure of community institutions upon which a more stable community can be built.

It is recommended that the University be broadly committed in favor of UCSB involvement (in Isla Vista)**. . . .**

<u>Specifically</u>**: that the Chancellor of UCSB take immediate steps to create an administrative office, properly staffed, to implement a policy of UCSB involvement . . . . utilizing the funds allocated by The Board of Regents on September 19, 1970, for the purpose of providing a community affairs officer and other services.**

Additional funding should be provided by the Regents as necessary.

COMMENT: The regents initially allocated several hundred thousand dollars. Most of these so-called Regents Funds went to policing and administration, but an important chunk went to nurture the development of several community institutions including the Isla Vista Community Council (IVCC), Open Door Medical Clinic, Community Federal Credit Union, Youth Project/Children's Center, etc. See the chart on page 49.

However, Chancellor Robert Huttenback's administration (1979-86) took the view that this was intended as "seed money" rather than as funds to be provided "as necessary" as the Trow Report explicitly recommended, and all of this funding was discontinued in 1983 -- without advance warning to these community agencies and without any Regent-level debate.

Even before 1983 the UCSB Administration was backing off its commitment to the community. Note that for the period 1976-1982 the allocation to the UCSB Administration to administer UC Regents funding of Isla Vista community programs exceeded the total distributed to community-run agencies (CC plus C) and that for the three-year period 1983-85 the UCSB Administration allocated over $85,500 to itself for administering no programs.

. . . we recommend that the Chancellor appoint a vice-chancellor who shall advise him on policies and decisions regarding Isla Vista, and who shall administer programs established there.

COMMENT: The title of the Vice Chancellor for Student Services had the words "and Isla Vista Affairs" added in 1970 and this position reported directly to the chancellor. This was maintained until 1975 when "Community Affairs" was substituted for "Isla Vista Affairs." There was no explanation offered as to why this change was made.

Branches of this office [Vice-chancellor of Isla Vista Affairs] should be located both in Isla Vista and in the Administration Building close to the Chancellor.

COMMENT: For 19 years following this recommendation, this vice-chancellor and his staff chose to remain in the UCSB Administration Building on the Main Campus. In 1990 the UCSB Administration rented 3,000-square-feet of office space in the Isla Vista Open Door Medical Clinic's new building at 970 Embarcadero del Mar in Isla Vista. For several years, an outreach person from the Dean of Student's office had an office there and space was available for community meetings. The University also sublet some of this space to the County of Santa Barbara, which also sited an outreach person from the Third District County Supervisor's Office in this space. However, this arrangement was dropped when the University leased the rebuilt Bank of America building for a lecture hall and other uses in 2002.

RECOMMENDATION: This vice-chancellor must have authority to initiate and coordinate UCSB services that relate directly to Isla Vista.

Specifically: that UCSB work with community organizations to upgrade the physical condition of Isla Vista, and that UCSB help in the building of community institutions, including:

(1-4) work with community members in constructing new community institutions . . . protecting Isla Vista ventures in their efforts to become community institutions . . . , to make UCSB services to students available where they live (i.e., in Isla Vista), . . . continue UCSB's active role in the development of the Isla Vista Community Center . . . (and) develop similar student-oriented services as new or different community needs become clear.

COMMENT: Initially, Regents Funds and a small grant from the Bank of America funded several programs that were able to rent out most of the space of the two buildings at 966 & 970 Embarcadero Del Mar in Isla Vista.

Today, 966 contains several commercial operations including The Cantina Restaurant, while 970 was purchased by the Isla Vista Open Door Medical Clinic in 1977 with a grant of federal funds allocated by the County of Santa Barbara and secured by the IVCC (see Chapter 11). These buildings together became known as the "Isla Vista Community Service Center," what the Trow Report called an "Isla Vista Community Center."

During the mid-1970s, while IVCC was attempting to secure funding to purchase both buildings for the bargain price of $140,000, the UCSB Administration twice refused to contribute $50,000 to the project — once from a student registration fee surplus that at the time was over $4 million. The recommendation from a student committee to allocate $50,000 of this surplus to purchase the Isla Vista Service Center buildings was vetoed by then-Chancellor Robert Huttenback.

The community was lucky to wind up with one of the buildings, which was purchased with federal Housing and Community Development funds through the County when Jim Slater was supervisor (1972-76), but for a price of $105,000.

The University funded the IVCC from 1971 through 1982. Over the period, the amount withered from $25,000/year to $9,000 and was terminated entirely in 1983 with less than one month's notice.

Beginning in the late 1980s, the University Administration and County officials began listening more to "The Federation", a loose coalition of interest groups (landlords, business owners, homeowners, a particular church, plus organizations with elected representatives such as the I.V. Park Board, the

UCSB Associated Students' Legislative Council, and, for awhile, the IVCC). Federation membership was appointed by the sitting County supervisor at the time, former I.V. resident Bill Wallace.

In 1972, and with the support of the UCSB Administration, County supervisors had recognized the IVCC as a "Municipal Advisory Council" — the official advisory body for Isla Vista residents (including those who lived on campus) to the County. Practically speaking, this role was supplanted by The Federation in the late 1980s. In the 1990s, when the Isla Vista Redevelopment Agency was established by the County of Santa Barbara, the Federation model was adopted for selection of membership on the Project Advisory Committee (vs. having an elected PAC). As was the Federation, PAC membership was dominated by propertied interests.

The IVCC went inactive in 1987, with its members feeling that neither the County nor the UCSB Administration was listening to the community's elected leadership.

RECOMMENDATION #2. That UCSB both initiate and seek the cooperation of others in initiating programs to create a more varied community in Isla Vista.

Rationale: UCSB should take the lead in working with residents of Isla Vista to develop a community marked by a greater diversity of age, occupations, interests, and other personal characteristics.

Specifically: the University should actively investigate the feasibility of establishing one or more small residential colleges in existing housing in Isla Vista, and it should locate in Isla Vista more UCSB cultural and academic activities.

COMMENT: The first recommendation was never followed, and the second exists to the extent that UCSB began some of these suggested activities in 1988 after they purchased the Magic Lantern Theater in Isla Vista and changed its name to the Isla Vista Theater. It is used primarily as a lecture hall, but it does have movies and some live entertainment several evenings per week. In 2002, the University leased and remodeled the rebuilt Bank of America building and converted it into a lecture hall with some space for studying and meetings. See the comments of Chancellor Henry T. Yang on page 164.

Specifically: the University should construct apartments (attractive to students with children) in Isla Vista or on parts of its campus adjacent to that part of Isla Vista in which most UCSB students live, (and) encourage faculty members and University employees to live in Isla Vista and to become involved with students and others in community.

COMMENT: Since 1970, UCSB constructed only the new married students housing project, but on Storke Campus not on the Main Campus as recommended in the Trow Report.

In the 1980s, the IVCC urged the administration to site its new faculty housing project on Main Campus, on the bluff adjacent to Del Playa Dr. The I.V. Park District even offered to trade some land in Isla Vista for the project for exactly the reasons suggested in the Trow Report. Instead, the project was sited on a large section of open space on UCSB's West Campus, because the bluff top on main campus was "too pristine" for a housing project. A few years ago, the university put up a student dorm complex holding 800 residents on the bluff top property.

RECOMMENDATION #3. That UCSB, the County, and members of the community cooperate to develop programs to provide increased and improved services in Isla Vista.

Rationale: **Many forms of municipal services are deficient or completely lacking in Isla Vista. Specifically: the University should give immediate attention to establishing greater UCSB-County cooperation — in the context of Isla Vista community involvement — to provide appropriate services for Isla Vista . . . .** (especially) **to develop and staff park and recreational facilities in that area of Isla Vista most heavily populated by students.**

COMMENT: In 1974, UC Regents' funds began being supplemented by county revenue sharing funds for social services and general funds for the IVCC. I am not personally aware of any major UCSB involvement in this process; primarily it was these fledgling organizations finding new resources on their own.

However, there was major assistance from the university in the purchase and development of Aniso'Oyo Park in the center of Isla Vista (1975). Although the bulk of the funds for the $480,000 project came from the federal government, the UC Regents contributed about $50,000; then UC Regent Norton Simon personally contributed an additional $69,500.

And UCSB loaned its campus planner for two years to the IVCC's planning department (1971-73). During his tenure, John Robert "Bob" Henderson taught dozens of UCSB students and local residents basic land-use planning and how these might apply in Isla Vista. He also assisted in the development of a community plan, which was published in 1973 as recommendations for Isla Vista planning, and designed Anisq'Oyo Park. See page 82.

After almost no involvement in Isla Vista from 1983 through 1988, a new initiative began in 1989 with the opening of a campus/country/community office in the Isla Vista Open Door Medial Clinic's building. UCSB had a full-time liaison in charge of new programs in the community. However, this operation was moved to Embarcadero Hall when it opened in 2002.

In addition, the County added an administrative assistant to the Third District Supervisor in late 1989. This person worked out of the UCSB office in the Isla Vista Medical Clinic building. In filling the position, County Supervisor Bill Wallace bypassed the County's usual personnel policies, instead designating one of his long-time campaign workers.

RECOMMENDATIONS #4 & 5. Increase the effectiveness of policing in Isla Vista
[paraphrased: C.L.].

Rationale: . . . . Repetition of the violence of the past would seriously undermine the potential effectiveness of all of our recommendations, which ultimately seek to build a sense of community. Should violence recur in the future, however, it must be met effectively and in ways that minimize the creation of hostility among the vast majority of Isla Vista residents who do not engage in violent acts. We believe that innovative approaches and procedures to police problems in Isla Vista are needed.

Specifically: that UCSB, local police forces, and community representatives immediately create a police liaison committee for Isla Vista to be charged with developing plans for dealing with major disorders, . . . that the University encourage community involvement in actual policing activities (and) . . . that the proposed police foot patrol in Isla Vista be implemented . . . as soon as possible.

COMMENT: It is with policing activities that one could say the university and the County have best cooperated to fulfill the recommendations of the Trow Report. The County sheriff secured a federal grant to commence a foot and bike patrol operation in late 1970. The university paid for half of this innovative policing operation from UC Regent funds. The Foot Patrol continues through today.

However, funding for UCSB's share was shifted from administration monies to student fees under Chancellor Robert Huttenback (1977-86). Acting-Chancellor Aldrich phased it back to administration sources over three years beginning in 1987.

The University for many years funded "Community Service Officers", non-sworn, unarmed personnel that are charged with some of policing traditional functions, but who cannot apprehend suspects. This promoted some confidence in the policing function among Isla Vista residents.

Trow Report recommendations not followed include the active recruitment of Isla Vista community members for sworn personnel, and some kind of empowered police/community committee to review police activities. However, the IVCC had a very active police commission for most of the 1970s, although it seldom had any cooperation from the police.

In addition, between 1977 and 1987, the sheriff reported to IVCC's public meetings about policing activities in Isla Vista for each month. After the IVCC disbanded, the Sheriff's department worked with the Isla Vista Federation. In recent years, the Foot Patrol has irregularly reported at Isla Vista Park Board meetings.

RECOMMENDATION #6. That the University provide recreational and housing facilities for Isla Vista residents.

Specifically: that UCSB should . . . formulate a standard lease though the cooperative efforts of UCSB, students, and Isla Vista property owners and managers, with a view toward reaching

172

an agreement adopted by all major landlords in Isla Vista.

COMMENT: Although some work was done on this project, such a lease still does not exist as of this writing (2008) according to the UCSB Community Housing Office.

Specifically: that the University develop contingency plans for additional apartment-style housing on campus . . . (and) encourage and assist interested community groups in the formation of student housing cooperatives . . . .

COMMENT: There was minimal activity on these recommendations for years. Only the new family student housing and the Santa Ynez complex on Storke Campus were added in the 1970s. Then nothing much happened in the 1980s and 1990s.

The University did help maintain and expand the Rochdale Housing Co-op after it was started by students. However, soon after it became involved, the Administration converted it to a student-only program — hardly in line with this recommendation.

To be fair, the University has significantly expanded university-owned housing in recent years. Initially the University bought two large apartment complexes in Isla Vista and converted them to student housing in the late 1980s, which hold about 575 residents. In about 2005, they bought Francisco Torres Residence Hall on El Colegio Road at Storke Road, which holds 1,325 UCSB students, and changed its name to Santa Catalina Residence Hall.

However, all of this additional housing is restricted to student occupancy, which certainly violates the intent of the Trow Commission recommendation. In addition, this has taken housing for nearly 2,000 people out of the private sector available to non-students, so it hasn't really taken pressure off the limited supply of housing in Isla Vista.

Other additional student housing projects include the Manzanita Village (800 students) on the bluff top on Main Campus near Isla Vista and the just-opened San Clemente Residence Hall (964 students) in what were once open playing fields along El Colegio Road.

Still, because UCSB student enrollment has increased by 8,884, or 71%, since 1973 (from 12,526 to 21,410 in the fall of 2007 according to the UCSB Office of Budget and Planning), there is a real question as to whether these efforts have been sufficient. These additional dwelling units have absorbed only 40% of the added students and only 10% (3,652 of 35,536) of the total population impact of this additional enrollment, when the multiplier effect is factored in. Note: UCSB's 1974 Long Range Development Plan estimated that an additional three-to-four persons are added to the local population for each additional student (8,884 x 4 = 35,536).

For an in-depth look at how UCSB enrollment practices have impacted Isla Vista, see pages 62-65 and Chapter 14.

Specifically: that the University use portions of the main campus adjacent to Isla Vista for

parks and playing fields (because) . . . efforts must be made to blend the dead-end streets of Isla Vista into the campus so that the feeling of a barrier now present there is eliminated . . . (and) priority should be given to construction of the projected University Student Center . . . adjacent to Isla Vista.

COMMENT: Neither of these recommendations was followed, although there is some talk of melting the Eucalyptus Curtain in the new Long-Range Development Plan currently under review.

RECOMMENDATION #7. That in view of the present level of services available to UCSB and Isla Vista, we believe the optimum size of student population has been exceeded. And until such time as our recommendations can be implemented and their effected evaluated, the present size of the student body should be maintained.

COMMENT: The Trow Report has never been evaluated by the University of California as to which, if any, of the report's recommendations were adopted, and what, if any effect the recommendations might have had.

In 1983 IVCC asked the UC Regents to establish a committee to undertake such a review. This request was denounced before the Regents by then-Chancellor Robert Huttenback as a "red herring." UC President David P. Gardner (by coincidence, a vice-chancellor at UCSB in 1970) did not support such a review. The Regents never voted on the request; basically, they just ignored it.

Of course, UCSB has not maintained its enrollment -- it grew from 13,733 in 1969 to 19,082 in 1989 alone and the 2010 Long Range Development Plan currently under review calls for an enrollment of 25,000 by the year 2025.

RECOMMENDATION #8. That the University-wide Administration take action to provide resources to UCSB to implement the recommendations of this report.

Rationale: Both the University-wide administration and UCSB have failed to muster and use the resources available to them to anticipate and to meet the problems in Isla Vista. We believe that the planning of UCSB as a campus and in its relation to Isla Vista has been inadequate and that immediate action must be given to taking actions that will guard against the repetition of past mistakes.

COMMENT: These funds were made available for the years 1970-83, then abruptly terminated. See the enclosed chart on page 49.

FINAL COMMENT: Overall, it's fair to ask whether UCSB has continued to take "actions that will guard against the repetition of past mistakes"?

APPENDIX B

BOB POTTER'S SPEECH
AT THE CEREMONY DEDICATING
THE MONUMENT
TO THE WORLDWIDE PEACE MOVEMENT
DURING THE VIETNAM WAR ERA
IN ISLA VISTA'S PERFECT PARK,
JUNE 10, 2003.

A third of a century ago, our forefathers…and foremothers —and fore-motherfuckers—hippies and yippies; speed freaks and Jesus freaks;

UCSB Professor Bob Potter giving this speech on June 10, 2003. Potter was the chair of the Perfect Park Monument Implementation Committee and the co-author of <u>The Campus By the Sea Where the Back Burned Down</u> (1970), a report to the President's Commission on Campus Unrest on the disturbances in Isla Vista and at UCSB, 1968-70. Photograph courtesy of Robert Bernstein.

Students radicalized by their professors; Professors radicalized by their students; Anarchists, Pacifists and Registered Republicans; Flower Children, Franciscan Friars and pissed-off Football Players; Marxist-Leninists and Proto-Feminists; Surfers, Sorority Sisters and Sexual Revolutionaries; Space Cadets and Vietnam Vets; the Hare Krishna and the Woodstock Nation; Visionaries in all colors and Mindblown lead guitarists of non-existent bands; not to mention winos, transients, alcoholics Anonymous and Otherwise, the Chairman of the Sociology Department and ordinary college students caught up in the pure adrenaline of the moment —

All of these people, and indescribable hundreds more, made history with their asses, by sitting down on them here in Perfect Park, in violation of a Police Curfew Order, linking arms to defend their community.

What could have brought so many unlikely people — including more than a few still alive here in this audience — to that outlandish act of defiance? Tonight, exactly 33 years later, it is worth looking back briefly, and as unsentimentally as possible under the circumstances, to remember what a hell of a mess things had gotten into.

To begin with, there was the **Vietnam Crisis**. By early 1968, with the February Tet Offensive, the American public had begun to wise up to the fact it had been lied to (does that sound familiar?) and that the Vietnam War had become unwinable, though young Americans continued to be drafted and killed in action by the thousands. This quickly brought on a **Political Crisis**, as President Lyndon B. Johnson was driven from the race in that Presidential Election Year by antiwar activists led by Eugene McCarthy and later Bobby Kennedy — whose assassination after the California primary in June brought chaos and deceit in its wake, a tumultuously rigged Democratic Convention and a bloody police riot in the streets of Chicago. And this coincided with a perilous turning point in the **Racial Crisis** in America. The non-violent insurgence of the Civil Rights movement to overturn segregation ended in calamity, with the murder of Martin Luther King on April 4, 1968, touching off catastrophic urban riots across the country, and calls for Armed Struggle. The backlash from all of this brought the election in November of Richard Nixon as President of the United States.

> *To begin with, there was the Vietnam Crisis. By early 1968, with the February Tet Offensive, the American public had begun to wise up to the fact it had been lied to (does that sound familiar?) and that the Vietnam War had become unwinable, though young Americans continued to be drafted and killed in action by the thousands.*

It was in the long shadow of these events that activism — violent and non-violent — came to the sunny shores of Santa Barbara. Thanks to the EOP program, an early example of Affirmative Action, the previously lily-white UCSB campus was integrated — though the Black students who arrived were unhappy enough with their treatment by campus bureaucracy and local law enforcement that one day they took over North Hall — the campus Computer Center! That every bit of the campus' computing went on in one small building tells you how long ago that was. The peaceful settlement worked out by the UCSB administration, brought the promise of more minority faculty and students, and new Black Studies and Chicano Studies Departments— but triggered a vicious denunciation from Governor Ronald Reagan, who had won his job in the first place by attacking student demonstrators at Berkeley, an ongoing **Educational Crisis**.

Concurrently an **Environmental Crisis** had erupted, with the Santa Barbara Oil Spill of January 1968, the single worst ecological disaster of our times, and the opening gun in a war of attrition between developers and environmentalists that continues along this coast to this very day. The oil-soaked dead birds on the beach turned surfers and ordinary beach goers overnight into radical activists.

Meanwhile, thanks to the baby boom, UCSB had doubled its enrollment between 1954 and 58, doubled it again by 1963, and again by 1967. Too busy building classrooms to bother with dormitories, the University solved its problems by steering this avalanche of students into substandard overcrowded apartment houses thrown up overnight by private land speculators and slum landlords, creating a demographic dystopia called Isla Vista, and precipitating a Housing Crisis (well, there's always a **Housing Crisis** in Isla Vista).

And all of this, let's remember, was unfolding generationally in the throbbing context of the **Countercultural Crisis** of the 1960's, that sexually-pioneering, musically-energized, chemically-induced metaphysical vision quest and psychedelic light show. Oh, you should have been here!

> *UCSB had doubled its enrollment between 1954 and 58, doubled it again by 1963, and again by 1967. Too busy building classrooms to bother with dormitories, the University solved its problems by steering this avalanche of students into substandard overcrowded apartment houses thrown up overnight by private land speculators and slum landlords, creating a demographic dystopia called Isla Vista.*

But if you were, you'll remember the pain and disillusion of it too. Woodstock led on to Altamont. Repression and violence were as American as Apple Pie, as Black militant H. Rap Brown pointed out. There were signs of trouble locally as early as 1969, with the arrest of 7 Black student leaders by the Santa Barbara Sheriffs on the pretext of an eviction notice, bringing student demonstrators out by the thousands. And April of that year brought the first death, when a bomb set off in the Faculty Club killed an innocent custodian, named Dover Sharp — a senseless violent crime still unsolved.

> *There were signs of trouble locally as early as 1969, with the arrest of 7 Black student leaders by the Santa Barbara Sheriffs on the pretext of an eviction notice, bringing student demonstrators out by the thousands.*

In the fall came news of the firing of a popular (and decidedly countercultural) Anthropology professor. The **Bill Allen Crisis**, which culminated in massive demonstrations and a petition signed by 7,776 students demanding an open hearing on his personnel case, was at once a carnivalesque assault on academic pomposity and a serious protest against the ivory tower obliviousness of much of the faculty, at a time when the world seemed literally to be coming apart. Bill Allen had the temerity to speak to students about what was on (and in) their minds, and it seemed he had been fired precisely for doing so.

And speaking of injustice, there were nightly TV news clips of the bizarre show trial of the Chicago Seven, with Judge Julius Hoffman railroading criminal Conspiracy charges against antiwar activists who barely knew one another, with Black leader Bobby Seale gagged and bound in the courtroom. At the

177

year's end, as Tom Hayden, one of the defendants, came to speak on campus, a **Crisis of Justice** was palpable across America. Could we trust our traditional institutions, or were they in the process of failing us, precipitating anarchy and revolution — or maybe fascism?

It was in such incendiary times that **Isla Vista** burst into flames 33 years ago, putting this most improbable trouble spot on the world map forever after. In the first few months of 1970 there were to be three major civil disorders.

In January came huge campus protests against the firing of Bill Allen, and the calling of Santa Barbara Sheriffs to clear the Administration Building of protestors, with Captain Joel Honey, the loose cannon of the Sheriffs Tactical Squad, leading the

> *. . . a Crisis of Justice was palpable across America. Could we trust our traditional institutions, or were they in the process of failing us, precipitating anarchy and revolution — or maybe fascism? It was in such incendiary times that Isla Vista burst into flames 33 years ago, putting this most improbable trouble spot on the world map forever after.*

charge. As Allen's appeal for an open hearing was turned down, with the arrest of 19 student leaders, matters careened off campus and out of control. On February 26, after a rousing speech by William Kunstler, the lawyer for the Chicago Seven, and the beating of student leader Rich Underwood by police, crowds gathered in the Isla Vista streets and attacked Realty Offices and the Bank of America, seen as the prime local symbol of the Establishment. Later that night, having chased off the police presence, the crowd set a fire in the lobby of the bank and then watched in amazement as the place burned to the ground.

The ashes of the bank were still smoldering the next day as Governor Ronald Reagan arrived in town to vilify the bank burners as "cowardly little bums" and call in the National Guard. The Bank of America took out nationwide full-page advertisements offering a $25,000 reward for the arrest of the arsonists, vowing to rebuild the bank. Reagan's call for a campus crackdown seemed to be heeded shortly afterwards, when Chancellor Vernon Cheadle banned Chicago Seven defendant Jerry Rubin from speaking on campus, saying it would "seriously threaten the welfare of the University." Unappeased,

Reagan made a speech to a Growers Convention on April 7, in which he made the following infamous statement about campus disorders: "If it's to be a bloodbath, let it be now."

It seemed he didn't have long to wait. On April 16, after a campus speech by Berkeley radical Stu Albert calling on students to "rip off the pigs," there was an angry rally in Perfect Park, then a vacant lot at the end of the Embarcadero loop that had become an informal community gathering place. As night fell the new temporary bank was attacked, as were realty offices; other students — protesting the violence— defended the bank and extinguished fires. The police waded into the middle of this melee, firing tear gas and birdshot into the crowd indiscriminately, from dump trucks specially outfitted for the occasion — an action that was dubbed "Operation Wagontrain". The next night the violence (and the resistance against it) resumed — with tragic consequences. As police arrived in riot gear, amid reports of sniper fire, anti violence students were attempting to defend the temporary bank from assault. One of them, Kevin Moran, was shot and killed.

KCSB the campus radio station was covering these events live, with reporters in the field, as they had in previous demonstrations. Fearing that the reports were giving away police tactics and deployments, Sheriff James Webster demanded that the University authorities close down the station — an order with which Vice Chancellor Steven Goodspeed complied. So it was that the only recorded silencing of a radio station by government order in American history took place, right over there on the UCSB campus. The death of Moran was attributed to snipers, and a dawn-to-dusk curfew was imposed, with heavy police patrols and reports of beatings and apartments broken into. On April 20, as Governor Reagan made a speech blaming Moran's killing on those who "take the law into their own hands," it was revealed that a Santa Barbara policeman had admitted that his rifle had "accidentally" discharged at the time of Moran's shooting. In a subsequent Coroner's inquest, held with little public scrutiny, the shooting of Kevin Moran would be ruled to be accidental, and the policeman, Officer David Gosselin, exonerated and returned to duty.

KCSB the campus radio station was covering these events live, with reporters in the field, as they had in previous demonstrations. Fearing that the reports were giving away police tactics and deployments, Sheriff James Webster demanded that the University authorities close down the station — an order with which Vice Chancellor Steven Goodspeed complied. So it was that the only recorded silencing of a radio station by government order in American history took place, right over there on the UCSB campus.

As universities across the country began to close down, the UCSB faculty was energized at last, moving quickly and effectively to keep our community together, by offering special "national crisis" courses focusing on the circumstances of the times.

Less than two weeks later President Nixon astonished the world, escalating the Vietnam War by invading Cambodia. The resulting firestorm of protest spread from coast to coast. At Kent State, Ohio National Guard troops fired into a crowd of protesting students, killing 4 of them. UCSB students occupied and closed the Santa Barbara airport, and surged onto the 101 Freeway, blocking it for many hours. As universities across the country began to close down, the UCSB faculty was energized at last, moving quickly and effectively to keep our community together, by offering special "national crisis" courses focusing on the circumstances of the times.

It seemed that the school year might end quietly, but events intervened once again. On June 3 news leaked out that 17 people — student leaders and activists, the "usual" suspects — had secretly been indicted, accused of burning down the Bank of America. One of those indicted had in fact been in jail the night of the bank burning. The resulting outrage led to further street and campus demonstrations, including attempts to torch the temporary bank. With disorder in Isla Vista once again, State officials, apparently acting on instructions from Governor Reagan's office, ordered the Los Angeles County Sheriffs to dispatch their Special Enforcement Branch to restore order. Instead, this notoriously violent paramilitary outfit, which had cracked heads in many urban riots, brought a reign of terror into Isla Vista. On June 8 and 9, enforcing a dusk-to-dawn curfew, the LA Sheriffs, accompanied by local law enforcement units, kicked down doors, dragged Isla Vistans from their houses, beat them bloody with their nightsticks, sexually harassed and intimidated, destroyed vehicles and personal property, sprayed mace and threw tear gas canisters into private yards and dwellings, threatening to shoot to kill.

. . . the Los Angeles County Sheriff dispatch[ed] their Special Enforcement Branch to [Isla Vista to] restore order. Instead, this notoriously violent paramilitary outfit . . . brought a reign of terror into Isla Vista. On June 8 and 9, enforcing a dusk-to-dawn curfew, the LA Sheriffs, accompanied by local law enforcement units, kicked down doors, dragged Isla Vistans from their houses, beat them bloody with their nightsticks, sexually harassed and intimidated, destroyed vehicles and personal property, sprayed mace and threw tear gas canisters into private yards and dwellings, threatening to shoot to kill.

At this very dark moment came Isla Vista's finest hour. With their streets under siege the next day, June 10, a group of faculty, student and community leaders met in the Methodist to seek a collective strategy. They decided to organize a sit-in in Perfect Park that night, to protest the police repression. By the time of the 7:30 curfew a quiet and determined crowd of some 700 had gathered, including UCSB faculty and staff and students of all

At this very dark moment came Isla Vista's finest hour. With their streets under siege the next day, June 10, a group of faculty, student and community leaders met in the Methodist to seek a collective strategy. They decided to organize a sit-in in Perfect Park that night, to protest the police repression.

social and political persuasions. When the police began arresting them for curfew violations, they reacted with calm, non-violent acceptance in the tradition of Gandhi and Martin Luther King. At 9:20, with nearly 300 arrested, police ordered the remaining crowd to disperse. When no one moved, the police sprayed pepper gas from a machine directly into the crowd. Then, as the Santa Barbara *News-Press* described it the next day, "gas-masked deputies swarmed into the crowd, flailing their nightsticks

180

in all directions." Those arrested were hauled away to the still-unfinished New County Jail where many were subjected to further beatings, denied bail, abused, stripped naked, sprayed with mace and thrown into solitary confinement.

But a crucial moral point had been made. Judge Joseph Lodge ordered charges dismissed against all those arrested and, faced with an ultimatum from University officials, Governor Reagan agreed to end the curfew and withdraw the L.A. Sheriffs. Peace returned to the streets of Isla Vista. The promised bloodbath had been averted, and the task of creating new institutions for the Isla Vista community had begun.

In the aftermath of the 1970 riots, a whole array of community institutions came into being in Isla Vista. The IV Recreation and Park District would go on to become a dynamic force in the establishment of parks and other public venues for the first time, along with the dream of cityhood (with or without Goleta). The University began to provide funds, and pay belated if sporadic attention to its unruly stepchild; one tangible result was the IV Foot Patrol, putting officers into direct daily contact with the community. Also established were the IV Credit Union, the IV Medical Clinic (bringing the inimitable Dr. Dave Bearman to town), the Isla Vista Youth Projects, and the IV Food Co-op, which remain vital and highly-value institutions to this day. In short a true community was born, out of the courage and solidarity of the Perfect Park sit-in.

One of the 1,000 non-violent demonstrators in Isla Vista's Perfect Park being hauled off to jail on June 10, 1970. This Isla Vista Slide Show photograph was used in the campaign to raise money to build the monument in Perfect Park to the anti-war movement around the world.

It was in an effort to commemorate that event, and in a larger sense the spirit of peaceful protest that is the most important legacy of the Vietnam era, that some visionaries set out in the early 1990s to create a Monument in Perfect Park. They had to begin by saving the Park itself!

Perfect Park had been purchased in the 1970s by a Santa Monica doctor who wanted to build a Safeway Supermarket. Only the long Goleta Water moratorium prevented him from doing so. In 1992

— eleven years ago! — Isla Vista voters approved a referendum saving Perfect Park from the developers, and two years later the Park District bought the property. Carmen Lodise, the historian and unofficial *Alcalde* of Isla Vista, was probably the first to propose building a monument to the anti-war movement on the site. That Carmen was proposing it guaranteed that certain other people would oppose it — and so indeed they did. Critics denounced the whole idea as an attempt to glorify bank-burners and bomb-throwers, waste taxpayers' money and enrich unspecified cronies.

In 1995 — eight years ago! — the IV Park District decided to appoint a committee to study the issue, including both proponents and opponents. Against my better judgment (I had, after all, co-authored a book on the IV Riots) I applied to join it. Despite our disagreements we held some useful public forums and learned that the IV community generally liked the idea. Most thought it should be a positive symbol for Peace, to unite rather than divide the community.

When the committee was reconstituted in 1996 we adopted a mission statement that made clear our commitment to honoring peaceful protest. We further decided that the monument should be built with private donations rather than public funds — a noble idea, though easier said than done. And as for what the thing should look like, there were dozens of conflicting strong opinions. A consultation with the County Art Commission yielded the bright idea of a national design competition, which of course we couldn't afford to finance. Here the amazing people at the Fund For Santa Barbara came to our rescue in 1997, funding a $3,800 grant, which enabled us to reach artists all over the country.

> *. . . as for what the thing [monument] should look like, there were dozens of conflicting strong opinions. A consultation with the County Art Commission yielded the bright idea of a national design competition, which of course we couldn't afford to finance. Here the amazing people at the Fund For Santa Barbara came to our rescue in 1997, funding a $3,800 grant, which enabled us to reach artists all over the country.*

To vet the entries we appointed a Selection Committee of arts professionals and community representatives (including John Muir, a combat veteran of the Vietnam war, who is here today). In June 1998 — five years ago! — the committee picked 6 finalists, who were given $500 grants to build models of their proposed monument designs. The following year, as fund raising began with a goal of $20,000, we held three public exhibitions of the models, on campus and in IV, gathering input and reactions to the designs; Santa Barbara artist Colin Gray's design for a cluster of arches proved to be the public favorite. In May 1999 — four years ago! — our committee voted to recommend Colin's design be built, and the IV Park District Board accepted the recommendation, authorizing the monument to be built on Park District land here in Perfect Park. Now all we had to do was raise $20,000.

Thanks to a flock of small donations, and a few large ones (thank you, Michael Douglas, and Richard and Tekla Sanford, for your $1,000 checks!) plus two generous grants of $2,500 from the IV Community Relations Council of the UCSB Associated Students, we had by June of 2001 — two years ago! — raised some $13,000.

They say that everything changed after September 11, 2001. That was indeed the case with our project. Suddenly, with the war in Afghanistan, a Peace Monument began to seem like a timely idea, rather than an exercise in nostalgia. People who had written us off as a bunch of aging hippies began to understand what we were up to, and pay attention. In January Congresswoman Lois Capps lent her name and support to our effort, speaking at a campus gathering where Colin's model was displayed, with television coverage from KEYT. In May 2002 — just a year ago! — filmmaker and film critic Peter Biskind came to town to show his infamous documentary Don't Bank on Amerika and help us raise over $3,000, and someone found a stash of old Burning Bank Check Posters and donated them to the cause.

In January Congresswoman Lois Capps lent her name and support to our effort . . . with television coverage from KEYT. In May 2002 filmmaker and film critic Peter Biskind came to town to show his infamous documentary Don't Bank on Amerika and help us raise over $3,000, and someone found a stash of old Burning Bank Check Posters and donated them to the cause.

As the Bush administration began its push toward war with Iraq, our small Peace project rode the wave of public outrage and protest as the Peace movement came alive all across the globe. Daniel Ellsberg came to town and joined our honorary board of advisors, which by then included Dick Flacks, David Krieger, Tom Hayden, Marc McGinnis, David Smith and Terence Hallinan. In February of this year, as the war clouds gathered, the L.A. *Times* ran a prominent feature story on our project.

Daniel Ellsberg came to town and joined our honorary board of advisors, which by then included [UCSB Sociology Professor] Dick Flacks, [Nuclear Age Peace Foundation founder] David Krieger, Tom Hayden, [founder of the Environmental Defense Center] Marc McGinnis, [founder of the Haight-Asbury Free Clinic] David Smith and [San Francisco District Attorney] Terence Hallinan.

That same week, — less than four months ago! — still $9,000 shy of our new goal of $25,000, I picked up the telephone to find that I was speaking with someone who wanted the Perfect Park Peace Monument to be built — and had the courage and the money to make it happen. Thanks to that visionary donor — who has insisted on remaining anonymous! — we received an astonishing pledge of $9,000 and broke ground in April.

So thanks to all the hundreds of people who made this possible — Diane Conn, Dave Bearman and Carmen Lodise still on the committee, and all the others who served time on it, including Mitch Stockton, Karl Brunner, Brent Foster, Dave Fortson, Leila Salazar, Ariana Katovich and untold others. And let's not forget someone whose reckless and disastrous actions put our initiative back on page one, and turned the Peace movement from a distant memory to an international necessity — President George W. Bush!

But finally our thanks must go to the people who, 33 years ago tonight, made a commitment to non-violence and kept it so memorably, who took a beating unflinchingly, looked repression in the face, and pepper gas in the eye — the people who made this ground historic when they put their asses on the line.

The wording on the plaque in the center of the monument reads:

In a spirit of remembrance, inspiration and reconciliation, we commemorate the people who worked for peace, justice and nonviolence in Isla Vista and elsewhere during the Vietnam war era.

The monument to the worldwide anti-war movement in Isla Vista's Perfect Park was dedicated on June 10, 2003, exactly 33 years after club-wielding police broke up a peaceful demonstration on this spot. These events are described here on pages 23-25.

APPENDIX C: PRIMARY SOURCES OF PHOTOGRAPHS

Several attempts to contact Ray Varley failed.

The Isla Vista *Free Press*.

I was the publisher, editor, and political writer for this weekly newspaper that was published 1987 through 1989. I took the photos not attributed to someone else. Note: Some original photos were lost and have been reproduced here from the website at lower quality.

Don't Bank on Amerika.

Many of the images of the events of 1969-70 in Isla Vista are from the movie "Don't Bank on Amerika," a 44-minute documentary by Peter Biskind, Steve Hornick and Jake Manning made in 1970. At the time, Biskind was teaching English at UCSB, but he left the following year. The film has become an underground classic and plays annually to sellout crowds in Isla Vista.

Peter Biskind during is 2002 visit to Isla Vista

Isla Vista *Free Press*. Left to right, front row: Keith Madigan, Photographer; a UCSB student intern; Fear Heiple, Entertainment Editor; Kelly Pritchard, Circulation. Back row: Gordon Harsaghy and Toni DiLeo, Advertising Sales; Rosemary Holmes, Artist; Carmen Lodise, Publisher; Sonya Holm, Layout & Design.

On June 10, 2002 Biskind visited Isla Vista and led an hour-long discussion following a showing of the movie at the Isla Vista Theater that benefited the monument to the worldwide peace movement during the Vietnam War era in Isla Vista's Perfect Park.

Biskind is a contributing editor to *Vanity Fair* magazine and the author of the best-seller Easy Riders, Raging Bulls: how the sex-drugs-and-rock 'n' roll generation saved Hollywood (1998).

Peter Biskind has given permission to use images from the movie in this book.

The Isla Vista Slide Show.

This one-hour, double-screened, narrated extravaganza was immensely popular in the mid-70s as part of the educational campaign about Isla Vista self-governance. Its principle artists were Eric Hutchens and Steve Logan. The project was donated to the community with a statement that there was to be no "ownership" involved. Lisa Pompa, Carrie Topliffe and Jeff Walsh updated it and nearly doubled its content in the early 1980s. Many of its 1969-70 images are from the movie "Don't Bank on Amerika."